WEALTH
&
HIGHER
CONSCIOUSNESS

Books by John-Roger

Passage Into Spirit
The Power Within You
Relationships—The Art of Making
  Life Work
The Signs of the Times
The Spiritual Family
The Way Out Book
You Can't Afford the Luxury
  of a Negative Thought
  (with Peter McWilliams)

Available through
MANDEVILLE PRESS
P.O. Box 3935
Los Angeles, CA 90051

WEALTH

&

HIGHER CONSCIOUSNESS

JOHN-ROGER

Mandeville Press ■ Los Angeles

Published by Mandeville Press
P.O. Box 3935, Los Angeles, California 90051

Printed by BookCrafters
Chelsea, Michigan
United States of America

I.S.B.N. 0-914829-51-3

Contents

Acknowledgments

I wish to acknowledge the following people for their loving assistance in creating this book: Rick Edelstein-Matisse, editor; Leslie Poling-Kempes, assistant editor; Betsy Alexander, copy editor; Holly Duggan, proofreader; Stede Barber, design and production; Ingrid Avallon, design consultant for dust jacket; Tom Mondragon, paste-up.

1

Choosing
Your Choice

"If you get anything from this book, perhaps the most valuable thing for you to learn is that you can create, promote, or allow everything in your life. Everything."

How do you get what you want?

First, you might figure out what you really do want. Some people want to get married; others, to get rich. Some want a joyous relationship with their mate and their children and an awareness of the Spirit within. Others want a new car, a new wardrobe, and a trip to Europe. And there are even some who want abundance on both the physical and spiritual levels (sort of an "on-earth-as-in-heaven" yearning).

Is it possible to get what you want? Yes, definitely. Although I do remember my mother once cautioning, "Watch out for what you want; you just might get it." I think that's still accurate. We *can* get what we want if we are willing to do those things that are necessary to get it. Many years ago, there was a legend that a person was discovered in a drugstore and made into a Hollywood movie star. I would guess that's more legend than fact. When you check the facts about those "overnight" movie stars, you'll probably find that most of them studied acting for many years and apprenticed in small roles on stage or in television and movies before getting the opportunity to be featured.

In other words, they spent many years struggling, sometimes going through severe financial deprivation, in order to refine their craft. Some worked as waitresses, bartenders, or taxicab drivers, but they never stopped focusing on their goal. Even though they may have gone with only four hours sleep a night, they still managed to study, rehearse, and live life with a single-mindedness of purpose. Those who did that—and stuck to it regardless of time or other conditions—had the greatest opportunity of making it. And many of them did. It's a matter of enduring to the end (the goal). It seems so simple, doesn't it? Figure out what you want, do what it takes to equip yourself to get it, and endure until you do. Are you willing to do that?

There is an expression: "There are no free lunches." That simply means that on some level or other, we have to pay for whatever we get. That's a fact of our economic system and, also, a process of the human condition. It could be to your advantage to accept that—not as a negative, limiting condition, but as information. With information, the best thing is to accept it and figure out how best to apply it in your life. In this particular case, it comes down to an important question: Are you willing to "pay the dues" to get what you want?

There are some major companies, whose gross income puts them at the top of American industry, that have personnel policies requiring every new applicant to start in the mail room and work their way up. Those who make it are willing to sacrifice, devoting themselves to learning and doing those things that work for them as they work their way up toward their goal.

Despite some sensational press releases, there are very few instant millionaires (except those who inherit

from their families). I know people who work regular
nine-to-five jobs, five days a week, and earn a moder-
ate income. I also know some very rich people who
work 10 to 14 hours a day, six to seven days a week. It's
a matter of choice and willingness to sacrifice immediate desires in order to get to the goal. Most successful people not only had to work very hard but had
to make sacrifices along the way. Was it worth it? To
some, yes; to others, no.

One of the key questions for you is, What am I willing to sacrifice to get what I want? Time with your family? Play time? Cut down expenditures in your everyday
life? Any choice can be all right. I know some people
who could have been millionaires, but they chose to
spend more time with themselves, their avocations, their
cultural interests, their spiritual expressions, rather than
sacrifice those for the focus necessary to build their
careers. I also know some very rich people who enjoyed
the focus and obsession of being successful.

You can, I repeat, most definitely get what you
want. The choice is yours. The naive person may "wish
upon a star" or hope to be "discovered in a drug store."
Mature people investigate, evaluate, and make deci-
sions about what they're willing to do and what they do
not want to do, and then they go on from there.
Choice, and more choice. Some people bemoan their
fate and blame the infamous "them" for their lack. If
they get truly objective, if they get high enough and
look at their lives with integrity rather than resent-
ment, they might learn that it isn't "them" out there
who stop their success. It is the "them" inside each person that is responsible.

If you get anything from this book, perhaps the
most valuable thing for you to learn is that *you can*

create, promote, or allow everything in your life. Everything. That's both the good news and bad news. It can be the good news if you take responsibility for your creations by behaving in ways that are cooperative and supportive. It can be bad news if you think that the only way of winning is to beat the other person and to be selfish and greedy. It is possible to win, experience great abundance, *and* assist others in winning. It is more than possible to experience the abundance in your life and the joy of spiritual awareness within you as simultaneous, connected experiences. In fact, if you are to gain those things you wish on this physical level—and enjoy them—I would guess that part of the success formula is to include a liberal dose of gratitude toward God, from whom all is granted.

Some of you may think, "Does God grant a new car?" Reasonable question. I am not suggesting that you dismiss your doubts. In fact, I think that you can use your doubt as a prover. At the same time, I'm not suggesting that you give in to the limitations of doubting, but that you let your doubt ask the question and you then seek the answer. It is not likely that God responds directly to your order for that new car, although Spirit may provide the opportunity for you to earn and save money for the car. Many people may pray for a new car, a winning lottery ticket, or a new washing machine. I suggest that you do not try to make God the "great bellhop in the sky."

I suggest that you use God for spiritual intention and that you permit Spirit to use you for loving success. I think that a valuable prayer might be asking Spirit to assist you in becoming more aware of Spirit. And then let Spirit do the rest. Of course, this prayer for awareness may be answered once, and then, in time, the awareness may dull and disappear. Why does that happen if God is omnipotent and omnipresent? Because we are living on a physical planet with distractions and temptations that lead us away from awareness of the Divine. So the prayer to become aware of Spirit, *constantly,* must also be supported with actions that permit Spirit to bring you loving and support. That's why so many people participate in spiritual exercises and meditation. They want to keep the channels open to awareness of the Divine.

There are some who have doubts about God. Does God really exist, or, if so, what does God do? How can someone really know, in a pragmatic, practical way, that there is a God, on a personal, individual level? After all, it seems that the age of miracles was in biblical days. Nowadays, it sometimes seems that it's a miracle just to get out of bed in the morning. I have heard people say things like, "If there is a God, the traffic light will turn green in ten seconds." Or when someone was lost, they prayed, "If there really is a God, I'll find my way."

Instead of giving in to these areas of superstition to try to prove the existence of the Divine, you can just go to your next breath. Who do you think breathes you? If you think it's you who are doing the breathing, use your doubt now and see if you can stop breathing. The Spirit in you takes your next breath, and Spirit also wakes you up in the morning. If you open to Spirit, you can access that divine energy to assist you in functioning on many levels, including going to work, saving your money, and even putting money down on a new car. You can use divine energy to improve your existence, and in that way, Spirit is definitely involved.

Then again, the cynic in you may say, "Well, is Spirit involved when I can't afford to buy that new car?" Sure, Spirit is involved in everything in your life, but it does not determine your income. You do. Spirit will support whatever you choose to do or choose not to do. "Whatever you *choose* to *do*" is a key to getting what you want.

Make your choice. Choose what you want—in reality, not fantasy. By that I mean that you can say you choose to win the Olympic decathlon, and here you are in your mid-thirties, overweight and living a sedentary, non-exercising life. That choice could be a fantasy. If, however, you choose to lose 15 pounds in the next three months, that's a choice with real possibilities because it can be accomplished on this physical level. If you choose to be a millionaire by the end of the week and you're currently unemployed, unskilled, and not doing anything about it, that choice is fantasy. If, however, you choose to double your income within the next five years, the chances are that you can make that a reality. How?

Choose your choice and focus on what you want. You decide where to put your consciousness. Some people make choices and then wait for them to happen, wait for "manna to fall from the heavens." Well, there have been great spiritual beings who could precipitate things from the heavens. Jesus, through divine forces, may have fed the multitudes with loaves of bread and fish, and Moses may have tapped into the divine forces by manifesting things on the physical level. For "ordinary" mortals, however, it is important to consciously choose our choices by doing supportive, practical things that work. Yes, you actually do have divine energy within you. Even so, there are things to be done on this physical level, using your mind, body, and Soul. I once heard a saying: "Pray to God, but continue to row to shore."

Focus the mental energy in the mind and loving energy in the heart *on your choice*. Make it foremost. Be aware, though, that there are positive and negative aspects to this approach. The positive elements are that as you do this, your mind has the opportunity to reveal possibilities as stepping-stones toward achievement; the heart can participate in support as you go for your choices with loving, wisdom, enthusiasm, and joy. The negative traps of this approach are that you might become so obsessed with your wants that you interpret everything as an obstacle and ride roughshod over it. If you express your greed by hurting others, the heart can close down. When you do not express consideration (to yourself and others) and you shut off the wisdom of the heart, your success is limited. You might get all the money you want, and you can also end up a miserable miser, best portrayed in *A Christmas Carol* by Dickens. Fear of his own death caused Scrooge to look into his heart. Scrooge finally did open his heart by sharing and giving, and so are these acts necessary to open the loving heart in real life.

If you are going to be obsessed with your wants, then make it a magnificent obsession. Within the magnificence is room for sharing, caring, supporting, and enjoying the process leading you to your goal. Permit your focus to inspire you, but do not overidentify with the awaited achievement lest you lose the joy of the process. It's not just a matter of the statement in the Declaration of Independence, "the pursuit of happiness," but also of the happiness of pursuit. There is an ongoing joy in the process. Some even think the process is more enjoyable than the achievement. For example, in sex that is actually lovemaking, the process of expressing tenderness lasts longer than the orgasm. If you go just for the goal without taking the time for the process, you may miss out on knowing that the pursuit of happiness is in the happiness of pursuit.

This is redundant, and it's still worth repeating: Keep your goal in the forefront and, simultaneously, involve your heart in the process; otherwise, you may achieve the goal without the joy of getting there. Ambrose Bierce once cynically defined *achievement* as "the death of endeavor, the birth of disgust." By keeping the enthusiasm of your heart involved and by recognizing that all things come through Spirit, your achievement can be just another part of the joyous process. Then, when you finally do get your new car, the experience is not over because, as you drive it, you can enjoy that experience as part of your ongoing success. When you do get that trip to Europe, you will know that everything that led up to it is also part of the trip. When you sit down for that expensive gourmet meal, your appetite is part of the enjoyment. When you consciously become aware of the Spirit within you after focusing on the Divine in spiritual exercises or meditation for hours, days, months, and years, awareness of Spirit is not just a payoff, but is an enrichment of the ongoing process you started way back when, and it continues into the future.

Part of choosing your choice and supporting your focus, your goal, is embracing a fundamental realization: *Prosperity is for you.* Some of you may have come from a cultural or family background that included limitations in the belief system. Within you may be an underlying theme that to be poor is to be loved or to be without is noble, or an unconscious programming of "since my parents were not abundant, abundance is not for me." Such limitations are not written in the heavens. If anything, *Divinity wants you to know joy and abundance as a reality.*

Accept this as a reality: *Prosperity is for you.* Then *make the decision* to *go for it.* Make the choice to choose it, to focus on it, and decide that not only do you deserve it but you're going to go for it and get it. Is that fantasy? If you indulge your doubts and just wish that prosperity would come knocking at your door, it may very well be fantasy. But if you are envisioning your prosperity and creating opportunities for opportunity to knock and open the door, it can be a positive reality awaiting manifestation.

In making your choice, focusing, and going for it, you will probably realize that this want/desire/yearning is number one in your mind, body, and heart. You may, by now, be aware that in the examples and techniques offered, there is a balance between the physical and spiritual. I know, by my experience and that of many thousands of others, that balancing Spirit and the physical level is not only possible and productive but necessary for enrichment, enjoyment, and success. When you awaken to and invoke the power of Divinity within you, you are also awakening to the power of Divinity within others. As you do that, you have access to energy sources that are so vast and powerful that your mind could boggle trying to understand it all. In fact, part of this process of manifesting your desires is beyond mental comprehension. Use the mind to focus, use the heart to perceive and support the higher actions, put your body on the line, and let the rest take care of itself.

Prosperity is for you — *both* the abundance of Spirit and the manifestation on this physical level. There is also an implied directive: *Do the best you can* and encourage others to *be the best they can around you.* That means colleagues, supervisors, students, those under your supervision, friends, lovers, mates, even clerks and waiters serving you. Many people think encouragement is a verbal expression, such as, "Go for it," to be delivered with inspiring enthusiasm. That is a more obvious form of encouragement. A more powerful support is not said with the voice but is stated in the heart and manifested in attitude.

Many forces come into play in order to manifest those things you want. It's like a magnificent jigsaw puzzle with thousands of pieces that you have to put together. Difficult? Sometimes. Simple? Yes. Easy? Sometimes, and often not. If you've ever worked jigsaw puzzles, you may remember that sometimes, after feeling frustrated, you finally found one piece, which opened things up for many, many more pieces to fit in easily. This is similar to solving the puzzle of creating what you want. You must find those key pieces that permit the others to fall into place easily. One of the most important "pieces" is attitude. If you create an attitude of supporting yourself and others in doing the best you and they can, many other pieces of your abundance can fall into line.

Many people think that wanting the best from themselves and others can often be demanding and

painful. It doesn't have to be. You don't have to demand or expect it. You can go for it with encouragement and enthusiasm. It's a matter of realizing that
prosperity and abundance are your rightful heritage.
Once you get that, it's a matter of recognizing that "going for it" is a matter of first doing the best you can,
which may not always be perfect. You don't have to
berate others or "get on their case" just because they
made a mistake. The key attitude is one of assisting
yourself and others in correcting yourselves on the way
to doing the best that can be done.

When you do that, you can ask for the spiritual
energy in support of your quest. You might call that
supportive energy *Light*. Light, the divine energy from
Spirit, is within each and every one of us. Whether that
energy is used for the highest good often depends on
our attitude. By choosing to choose, by focusing your
mind, body, and heart, by doing what it takes to do the
best you can, and by making a safe place for others to
participate with you as they do the best they can, you
can readily access the Light.

The Light can come forward not only from within
you but also from others you are encouraging and supporting, which, coincidentally, can support you. When
someone does the best they can do, the Light is present,
available, and accessible because the Light is the best
there is. If you fall short and choose not to get up one
more time than you fall, if you choose to settle for less
than what you can do, the Light will still be present,
but it may not seem as accessible.

By your attitude and actions, you can support
others in being the best they can be, and part of that
action is sharing your consciousness of prosperity. The

more energy you put into being aware that prosperity is yours to enjoy, the more likely you are to manifest prosperity on the levels you want. But this is not just a matter of words; it is a matter of sharing with consideration and cooperation. Once that Light in you is accessed and the Light in others is available, the formula for success includes showing it, using it, and sharing it.

People will be attracted to you as you show and share your Light, and they will come forward to contribute to your success. Greed is like the flame that attracts moths, which usually burn themselves out. But the spiritual Light, which exists within you, is like a divine magnet that will attract others who seek to share their own Light, expanding the source of your success. Some people may be frightened by this onrushing support and back away, wanting to remain in a more familiar level of limitation. If you want more than this, however, it means claiming the Light, the support, and the prosperity that are available and embracing success past your wildest dreams.

This may sound like an obviously easy thing to do. It *is* simple — but not always easy — because of the conditioning that says, "You can't have it all." If people have that as a conscious or unconscious belief, they will probably make sure they limit themselves. I know of two primary approaches that can assist people in transcending limited conditioning; in fact, these approaches can even transform them so the same energy of limitation can then be used for infinite expansion. These approaches are so valuable to me that I consider them my personal "commandments." I am not one of those writers who tell about the joy of spiritual and physical abundance just on a theoretical basis. I and many others share these commandments and, as a result, we experience the joy of abundance as an everyday occurrence. What are these two commandments?

1. Work and serve.

2. Learn and grow.

We have two minds in the world, one that is spiritual and the other that is material. The material mind is the one in which we work and serve. The spiritual mind is the one in which we learn and grow.

Working is a matter of putting your body on the line to complete a task. Some people work reluctantly, resistantly, and in a state of malicious obedience, doing exactly what they are told to do and using none of their own initiative, intelligence, or loving. Some may be so resistant that they keep from their colleagues or supervisors information that could improve the work. Obviously, that is not the kind of attitude I recommend, unless, of course, you want to increase your poverty and reduce your opportunities for prosperity.

The attitude I am talking about in relationship to work is one of *serving*. Inherent in serving is doing the best you can. That means making the choice, focusing on the task at hand, and using your mind, body, and Spirit—for the joy of doing it. Notice that I didn't say to do it for the money you will get at the end of the week or for any recognition or reward. If you work and serve with an attitude of enthusiastic cooperation, knowing that you are serving the Spirit within you by serving others through your work, you can receive incredible support for creating your abundance as a living reality.

Learning and growing are actually a manifestation of working and serving. What is there to learn? Everything. And if that seems a little overwhelming, how about learning not only to do the best you can but, each day, to let your best be just a little better? A proof of learning is the ability to handle life's situations—particularly the difficult ones—more easily. A validation of your growth is that what was once a difficult situation has now become as easy as breathing—just a matter of in and out, doing it until it's done, without the emotional charge that often creates resistance and limitations.

At the beginning of this chapter, choosing your choice is stated as a key to your success. You have to decide if you truly want success and are willing to do those things that succeed. Will you choose to work in resistance, or is your choice to work and serve as if that's your calling? If you choose to serve, you can become valuable to your boss, colleagues, and clients. Your earnings and your business and personal relationships will most likely expand because of this choice. Working, serving, learning, and growing are techniques, actions, and results that all point to getting what you want.

2

Is Faith Practical?

"I am interested in practical spirituality, that spiritual expression that manifests for use in our lifetime—not some far-distant future, but within the ongoing, day-to-day experiences of our lives."

I nherent in creating a consciousness of wealth—
which, indeed, can create wealth on all levels—is
the belief that you can create what you want. For those
of you who have done this, your belief is based on empirical evidence. If you have not yet created the wealth
you desire in your life, this belief, then, is actually a
matter of faith.

Faith is a much belabored word. It has been used
both positively and negatively. Faith can be used to
deter doubters from discovering the truth, with an attitude of, "Believe this without questioning or checking
it out." Faith can also be used to support doubters in
their search, knowing that the truth, once found, will
be valuable. The Bible states, "Faith is the substance of
things hoped for, the evidence of things not seen."[1] It
seems paradoxical—"the evidence of things not
seen"—doesn't it? The doubter asks, "How can you
have evidence of something you cannot see?" The
knower responds, "It may not be seen in terms of
physical vision, but I can see it in terms of my heart."
Another way of saying that might be, "I sensed it."

1. Hebrews 11:1 (King James Version)

Haven't you had many, many experiences of sensing something? When you knew in your heart that something would happen, that someone cared, that someone loved you, that you would succeed in some venture? Even such adages as "if at first you don't succeed, try, try again" are truths that can be verified only if initially acted upon in faith. When you fail, when you fall down, when you miss out on something, you can, of course, quit. And some people do. But if you do get up one more time than you fall, if you do correct yourself one more time than you make a mistake, success is waiting for you. How do I know? It's a matter of faith based on empirical evidence. Or as the New English Bible says, "Faith gives substance to our hopes, and makes us certain of realities we do not see." I appreciate that expression, "realities we do not see."

People are awakening to the greater realities, which, in actuality, are not seen with physical vision, but are seen, perceived, intuited, felt, sensed with the knowing essence of the Spirit within you. Part of the process of manifesting abundance and making it your own involves acts of faith. This is not just having faith that something good will happen; I'm not talking about wishing on a lucky star or betting your favorite number and having faith that you'll win. I'm talking about a faith that involves your doing those positive things that produce successful results.

If I say that thousands and thousands of people on this planet have claimed and manifested their prosperity, what would you want to know? You'd probably want to know how they did it so you, too, could have your share of prosperity. Part of this action has been stated previously: knowing that prosperity is not a distant thing that may or may not be attainable, but is available on the levels that *you make room for it*. For example, if you have a water well and it is filled with rocks and debris from years of neglect, when the rains come, there may not be enough room in the well to store this fresh, nurturing water. What is there to do? Clear out the rocks and debris before the rains come. Make room for the fresh water to cleanse and enrich your life.

Similarly, with yourself, you may have obstacles, your forms of rocks and debris accumulated unconsciously over many years, that block prosperity from flowing into your own well. If you do, you need to make room for prosperity to overflow within you, manifesting as *you* in a state of abundant wellness. "Physician, heal thyself" is an excellent suggestion. You are both the doctor and the patient, and the cure is within what you choose to do, or not do. Acts of omission are often as effective, if not more so, as acts of commission. For example, cleaning out your "well" on your way to wellness may mean removing blocks of improper diet and omitting sugar products or fried foods; it may mean omitting negative emotional responses; it may mean keeping silent instead of hurling invectives in anger and hurt.

Those aren't always easy. Once again, that's where faith comes in. It requires faith to do those things that will strengthen you to stop doing those things that weaken you. How do we produce a clear well within us that permits success to come forward on all levels (spiritual and physical)? First comes faith. And, once again, I'm not talking about the miraculous faith that parted the Red Sea or fed the multitudes, but something more pragmatic to the average person.

Everyone acts on faith, even those who may be reluctant to admit it. Have you ever sent away for something that was advertised in a catalogue? And I'll bet you even included a check or your credit card number to pay for it. You had faith that the product whose picture you saw would be delivered. I'm sure you can think of many experiences in your life where you acted on faith that something promised or something expected would happen. But in order to reap the benefits of it, you first had to act on faith. You first had to send in your order.

So it is in terms of clearing the channel within you for Spirit to support the manifestation of "your order." Each of us already has a success form working inside us. If you have had "rocks in the well," you may not have been in touch with this success form, and instead, it may be blocked, which often manifests as confusion and ambiguity. The task at hand is to clear away the rocks. An appropriate saying, at this point, is, "With enough loving, even the rocks will open." It's a matter of loving yourself enough to clarify and clear the channel so that your success can manifest in reality, in this lifetime, for you to have, enjoy, and share.

Manifesting material things is not that difficult, and I suggest that you don't consider that the end-all and be-all because of all the things that come with material manifestation. You may manifest that "dream house," and guess what else you have to manifest? The insurance, the air conditioning/heating system, the furnishings, and so on. What I'm focusing on in this book is not limited to physical manifestation. In fact, I am suggesting that physical manifestation has limited worth unless you awaken to and cooperate with a higher consciousness within you.

On a prosaic level, for example, if you manage to manifest that incredible car of your yearnings — that Porsche or that Rolls Royce or that convertible with a souped-up engine — you also have to cooperate with traffic laws in order not to have a collision and possibly hurt someone else or yourself. Well, shift that coopera- tion a thousandfold and you might understand that along with physical materialization comes something that will outlast your car (which has a built-in ob- solescence). Imagine cooperating with Spirit to such a degree that everything you do helps you and helps others, so that you never hurt yourself or anyone else, so that you use everything — I mean *everything* — for your advancement. If you focus first on your spiritual advancement, then all things "on earth as in heaven" can come to you. The Bible says, "Seek ye first the kingdom of God, . . . and all these things shall be added unto you."[2] The priorities are clear, and the process of manifestation is built in.

Manifestation of abundance through Spirit to this physical level requires many supportive steps, some previously described. You may have a vague idea of how to create something in your life. To transform a nebulous idea into a productive reality takes some specific work. Some people first choose to contemplate. They may "plug in" the idea, stare out a window, and just contemplate, seeing what comes forward. Others may do spiritual exercises, clearing the channel for spiritual inspiration. Others, once they have "plugged into" the idea, may intentionally do things that distract the conscious mind (listening to music, taking a walk), trusting that the subconscious will work on its own and

2. Matthew 6:33 (King James Version)

that Spirit will bring forth the clarity with the rested mind's cooperation. (Faith, again.) Still others may support the mind by using a simple step-by-step process of writing down all their ideas, rewriting until they are reduced to a few ideas (which may still be ambiguous), and then rewriting again until clarity is achieved. Some people go through a similar process by talking about their vague idea until they reach clarity.

The point is that from the often nebulous place of intuition, inspiration, or mentalization, the process involves taking an idea into a specific manifestation that can express your imagination and contribute to the betterment of your life and that of others. Artists know that process well, although it is mostly an emotional, intuitive process using their craft, not just a mental process. The artist responds to stimuli (inner and outer) with a subjective feeling and gives them form on the physical level, from painting to sculpting to poetry. So, too, are you an artist. In your case, perhaps the canvas is your life.

If you do nothing with your intuition, your inspirations, or your creative ideas, then you are choosing (by omission, perhaps) not to bring forth the manifestation of your potential. A lump of coal, left alone, is just that. If you set fire to that piece of coal, however, it transforms into a useful form of energy. (A diamond is a chunk of coal that made good under pressure.) The lump of coal had the potential for more than just sitting there, but potential obviously does not mean manifestation and availability now.

I am interested in practical spirituality, that spiritual expression that manifests for use in our lifetime — not some far-distant future, but within the ongoing, day-to-day experiences of our lives. When coal burns, it is released into a higher level of energy. From a base place, the potential is actually manifested as a higher expression. Similarly with you as an individual, there may be work to be done so you can express your potential. Too many people die with an unwritten epithet, "He (or she) had so much potential." I much prefer living with the credo, "I am expressing my potential now." Perhaps you can focus on the Light within you and increase the pressure, so the coal inside you can create enormous energy for you and can be transformed into that diamond, manifesting abundance from within, for you.

Know this: (1) All things, human and otherwise, have potential; (2) Everything and everyone is involved in the process of releasing to a potential. The good news is that there are opportunities for higher levels of expression. The bad news is that it is not necessarily releasing from the bottom up; it could be releasing from the top down. So, once again, it is a matter of consciously choosing and then doing those things that support your choice. Your activity can awaken you to the availability of your potential and can manifest positive, uplifting things in your life. It is important to recognize that potential exists in all states. In illness, health is a potential. So is death. In any problem lies the potential answer. Even in poverty is the potential of abundance. Within mortal human beings is the potential of the divine realization.

The beautiful thing about divine manifestation and abundance is that the potential is not restricted to any particular group of human beings. Regardless of which groups declare themselves elite or which groups interpret scripture to support their own particular Divinity to the exclusion of others, abundance through Spirit is available to all. As a matter of fact, claiming an elitist, exclusive right to divine energy can actually stop growth because containment and curtailment are in opposition to Spirit. Spirit is a constantly expansive, available energy that is not manipulated by interpretation, but is dynamically present. It is up to each individual to keep the "well" or channel open to receive of the blessings of abundance.

Your job, from a high point of view, is to keep dynamically open.

(1) This dynamic opening is what moves the energy from potential and makes it available.

(2) Then your focusing moves that which is available and makes it accessible.

(3) After that, it is a matter of continually putting your body, mind, and heart on the line so you can move the energy from accessible and make it a manifest reality.

All that action can be a product of tapping the potential of Light. Light might be an acronym for **Liv**ing **In** **G**od's **H**oly **T**houghts. This is an action that takes place through you — not just as a word or an elitist position or proposition, but as a manifestation of openness to the divine energy. As you create the opening, by letting go of such limitations as judgments, emotions, and ego, you create your own space for the source of power. There is an expression "By your acts you shall be known." Similarly, by your actions, you have the opportunity of accessing divine energy and using it to create abundance on many levels.

By your actions you can discover the reality of Spirit as a support system in your life. Such actions will validate the value and practicality of faith.

3

Eight Steps to Prosperity

"God doesn't care if we have money, and to know God does not require knowing poverty."

Let's talk about money. Of course, when I speak of wealth, I am talking about it on many levels, which include not only financial abundance but also an abundance of good health, mental alertness, emotional stability, and spiritual well-being. But for now, let's talk about money.

Nearly everyone on this planet is striving to make money. Not only that, but money often seems to be the thing many people's lives revolve around. Some equate their self-worth with how much money they can make. Some get more joy out of getting money than from relationships, sex, cultural events, sleeping, or eating. Take a look at the gambling centers of the world. In Las Vegas, for example, there are huge casinos that have room for thousands of people. In these casinos, devoted to money, are slot machines, baccarat tables, roulette wheels, tables to play blackjack or poker, but guess what they don't have. They don't have many windows, nor do they have many clocks. They do everything they can to support gamblers in suspending their usual reference points of time and place. That's an extreme, of course, but in other ways, people create their own "casinos" and go for the last dollar they can get.

We have heard people preach about the evils of money, and others preach for contributions of money. Some have even renounced money and the material world in favor of God. But God doesn't care if we have money, and to know God does not require knowing poverty. In fact, people can verbally renounce material possessions and money, but even they are stuck with some financial considerations as long as they are alive. They still have to pay for food, rent, taxes, carfare, and their electric bill. Of course, if you want to renounce money totally and still be alive, you might choose to live in deprivation and beg for food. I respect any individual's choice, but I doubt if you, who are reading this book, are interested in that lifestyle.

Since you are in a physical body and are bound by the laws of this physical universe, you may as well accept, cooperate, and get on with it. There are negative and positive aspects to this physical level, and you do have a choice as to which you will support. You can go for money out of negative greed, go for money on the basis of need, or go for money for the joy of what it can get for you and others. Using the latter as a guideline permits you to live on the physical level in abundance and, simultaneously, to move into the higher consciousness.

I grant that it is very difficult to do "spiritual" work when you are worried about car and house payments, insurance premiums, and gas, light, and phone bills. It's even more difficult to enjoy material wealth in health and happiness if your consciousness is not awakened to your divine source. It's a matter of having your feet firmly planted on the earth—and your head in the heavens. Prosperity, which means health, wealth, and happiness to me, must come from inside and then manifest outside in the world. You *can* live your own prosperity.

If you can apply what you have already read, you may have a rich, fulfilled life. In my experience, however, I find that people's minds, egos, and limited programming often resist change. Just as little children often have to be told the same thing many times by their parents or teachers, so, too, is there a childlike part in each of us, which has to be told things many times before we can effect a positive change in our behavior. It seems odd that there is such resistance to a life of prosperity, but, then again, the way many people choose to live their lives on this planet often appears odd to me.

Imagine, if you would, that God granted enough agricultural resources to feed all the people of the planet. Imagine that God granted all the natural resources to house everyone in a heated home with hot and cold running water. Imagine that God granted specific support for everyone to live in comfort and abundance. And then imagine that human beings choose to ignore those God-given gifts of prosperity and choose to live in doubt, deprivation, and conflict. Odd, isn't it, because *we do have all the natural resources for five billion people to live balanced lives.* Somehow, however, people have chosen to live in deprivation. Rather than give in to the oddity of the human condition, I'd sooner offer some specifics that can permit you to transcend limitations and claim your divine heritage: prosperity, otherwise known as health, wealth, and happiness.

What is the specific "magic formula"? It's only magic when you don't know how to do it. When you know, it's real. I'll spell out the *eight steps to prosperity*. Whether they become real to you or remain magic depends on whether you'll do the eight steps. It takes more than nodding your head or saying, "I agree with that, sure." It takes *doing*. It's as easy as—I was going to say, "A to Z," but let's call it "A to H."

A. Accept Your Opportunity

If your second cousin died and left you a million dollars, I doubt if you'd have difficulty accepting that opportunity. When I suggest accepting our opportunities, I am including the more subtle ones, even those that may appear to be negative. Sometimes we see or participate in an event and don't accept that it is, indeed, an opportunity. There is a conditioned part of us that often labels events to fit into our cultural or familial patterns, so that we can feel more comfortable with them.

For example, I know of a young man who went to kiss a young lady he cared for, and she turned away. Because he was hurt, the conditioned part of him lashed out, and as he expressed anger, he categorized her as an insensitive tease. The only thing is, she didn't have the same script he did. Her response had nothing to do with teasing or personal insensitivities. She told him, "I didn't kiss you because your breath smells so much of nicotine from smoking cigarettes that I get nauseated."

Is that a knock or an opportunity? He had tried to quit smoking numerous times, but was hooked on nicotine. In this circumstance, however, he was more hooked on kissing the young woman he cared for than on smoking cigarettes. So he used this as motivation to quit smoking. He not only got to kiss but, years later, he found out that if he had continued smoking, he might have developed emphysema or possibly cancer. He may not have consciously said, "Her rejection is my opportunity," but he used it for his betterment. He, by action, used the incident and information as an opportunity.

I have heard it said that opportunity knocks only once. In my experience, opportunity knocks, and knocks, and knocks in infinite ways. So if you "blow it" and mishandle something, if you didn't accept or recognize an opportunity, don't bemoan your fate. Just learn from the experience and do better next time.

Opportunities come in all shapes and sizes. How do you know if something is an opportunity or not? Frankly, I approach most moments in my life as opportunities. Even the negative ones? *Particularly* those events that seem like obstacles to my enjoyment of life. When I got a speeding ticket, I gave up speeding (like the young man who gave up smoking) lest I get cited for another moving violation, which would make my insurance go up considerably. Was that an opportunity? Sure, because who knows—maybe my speeding would someday have caused an accident that could have maimed someone, including me. It's not so much that I am grateful for the time I was caught speeding, but I am grateful that I accepted that as an opportunity to change my driving patterns.

If you hear a subdivision of *accept your opportunity*, you're right. It's called *choose your attitude*. There are many things you cannot choose, such as your parents, race, color, or place of birth. But you can very well *choose the attitude* with which you deal with them. You can wake up "on the wrong side of the bed" and still not give in to irritability. What is the opportunity? To recognize that, for some reason, you feel out of balance and to still *choose* to do those things that support you in prosperity, instead of giving in to the thing that can corrupt you. Expressing anger doesn't promote prosperity, but corrodes it. The challenge is to consciously put energy into a *self-supportive attitude* that says, "So what if I am a little irritable? I don't have to dump it on others. I'm still going to read the paper, meditate or contemplate or do spiritual exercises, eat a nourishing breakfast, and count my blessings rather than discount them."

I am not saying to lie to yourself and deny that irritability exists in you, but just to recognize that the ability to be productive, calm, and joyous exists in you at the same time. You're the one who chooses which to act on. If you promote negativity, guess what you'll have. Of course, negativity. I know many people who live a life of health, wealth, and happiness. None of them, not one, lives a life of consistently promoting negativity. Sure, you may slip here and there, and there is even an opportunity in slipping and falling down: you can get back up again. Getting back up means choosing what will support your positive prosperity, instead of giving in to the negative temptation of limitation.

If you focus on the negative long enough, you may fall into despair. If you do find yourself in the pits of despair, you don't have to remain there just because you may have been taught that is your fate. Now that you're an adult, how about taking a light with you? The Light of awareness, the Light of God, the Light that illuminates the traps so you don't have to fall into them. Is it that simple? It could be. It's a matter of what you focus on, like seeing a glass of water half-full or half-empty. Where is your focus?

You are born with freedom of choice. Particularly for people who live in societies where abundance and freedom are more accessible, choice is even more apparent. Imagine that you not only have the choice but even have the power to transmute a negative condition into one of positivity, sort of like an attitude-alchemist. I remember a story a friend told me about when he helped push a car out of a rut in the mud, in driving rain, yelling directions to the person driving. The wheel rotated, spurting mud all over his body, face, hair—everything. The car went nowhere, and he got totally soaked by the mud. He could have kicked and screamed, making the rain, the mud, the tire, and even the driver wrong. And he still would have been caked with mud. Instead, he looked at his reflection in a puddle, saw an "oozing monster" in himself, and broke up laughing, carrying on like a laughing idiot in the rain. It didn't get the tire changed, but it sure was fun. He knew he'd eventually get the tire changed. He knew it would eventually stop raining. How did he know? Perhaps it's called common sense, or "faithing." Putting energy into a positive focus that may be unseen at the moment and then moving your body toward it, is what I call *faithing*. It's a way of accepting your opportunity.

B. Begin to Go for It

I'm not suggesting that you blindly jump into something with false enthusiasm supported only by a slogan that says, "I'm going for it, and I'm going to get it." If you don't prepare yourself for whatever it is, all you might get is a lesson. And that's not bad, either, because it's another opportunity to learn that going for it can be a mature, conscious process. As it says in an earlier chapter of this book, figure out what "it" is. Determine what it is that you really want before you begin to go for it. You may want to get downtown in a hurry. The way *not* to go for it is to run onto the freeway and try to hail a car amid all that traffic. That's an obvious one, but I'm sure you get the point.

Figure out what cares and considerations you have before going for it. What are the things you have to do in order to begin? Our minds often do funny things when we're trying to change and progress, so I suggest that you make it easy for the mind by actually *writing down the steps* you think of, the things you have to do in order to begin. In this process, you may find that each step leads to the next one. If you don't know the next step, reevaluate your last step because it has within it the information leading to the one following it. It's also important to start with integrity, so that the very first step has a truth (as you perceive it), and to write each step with the same care.

A subdivision of beginning to go for it is to *believe in your ability* to do it. If I started this process by asking you to believe in your ability, you might end up with an empty slogan of belief. But if you follow this step-by-step process of accepting your opportunity, choosing your attitude, beginning to go for it by defining "it," and writing down the step-by-step approach, the likely result will be a solid belief in your ability because you will have already involved yourself in a feasible process that creates success.

In this process, do not avoid areas of discomfort, areas in which you feel confused. On the contrary, check out those areas to determine what it is that may confuse or frighten you. You don't have to jump into them and feel confused or afraid; just objectively check them out within you. Write down what you think you don't know, and ask for clarity. Ask whom? The knower within you. You may be surprised to find the answers coming forth and freeing you from fears and limitations.

What are some of the limitations? The times we may try to make our lack of success someone else's fault. And if we're not blaming someone else, we may blame something within us, as if we have no control over it. How many times have you not done something positive on the basis of, "I can't because I have a headache," or "I'm just not up to it today"? Then you might wonder why opportunity doesn't seem to knock at your door more often. If you have shut the door on small opportunities, the big ones may not come calling. Blaming someone (including yourself) does not improve your condition, so it's an approach that can simply be dropped. Why waste time on blaming if it doesn't get you what you want?

C. Commitment

You remember that A was *accept* and B was *begin*. Now, C is *commitment*. A powerful energy is inherent in committing. It may not allow for alternatives. Commitment is keeping your focus, your attention, and your awareness on what you have accepted and begun and then sticking to it with single-mindedness of purpose. When you commit, it is going to produce change. That sometimes frightens people because change may mean stretching their "comfort zones," going into unfamiliar areas of expression and experience. Even if these new areas are beneficial, many people resist change.

Change sometimes produces a feeling we may label as pain. Some people find it painful to give up areas of old, comfortable familiarity and to change aspects of their behavior. Some people even fear change so much that they commit negatively and condemn all opportunities for change and growth. It has been said that it takes great courage to see the face of God. If this is something you have committed to doing, you can strengthen yourself by developing the courage to support the positive choice rather than the negative one and by beginning to go for the positive changes that are available. It's like coming out of the cocoon and becoming the butterfly. The process of breaking loose may be momentarily uncomfortable, but you don't have to call it pain. You can change your attitude and honestly call it a wonderful opportunity, as you unshackle yourself from conditioned confinements and choose to move into freedom. What comes with that choice? Joy.

D. Devoted to Your Goal and Dream

If you have a vision, a dream, a yearning for something that is worthy of you, then it is also worthy of your devotion. What is worthy of you? That which uplifts you, supports you positively, and contributes to your joy and abundance. When you connect and commit to that, you can devote your life to it. And it's less a matter of your saying, "I'm ready to die for it," than your knowing, "I'm ready to live for it." I mean really *live* by experiencing the zest, the enthusiasm, the happiness of living in gratitude and fun. Devotion is an energy that prepares the way in a manner that is often unseen yet often results in incredible opportunities. Devotion is an energy that says, "Regardless of considerations, I will move on it, with it, under it, around it. No matter what, I will go for it."

Some people may hesitate to go for it because they reflect on the pain and deprivation in their lives. Why reflect on misery from your past? Here you are, right now, reading a book that says you are worth more, now and forever more. Whatever you did up to this point, let it be okay because here you are now, seeking a way to improve your life — not just to make it better than yesterday, but to actually create a life filled with prosperity. Any limited levels you have experienced up to now can even be regarded as valuable because here you are, right now, sitting in the lap of luxurious opportunity.

How will this opportunity present itself? For many, a change in attitude will clear the way. How about, as a subdivision of devotion, your willingness to *dare to succeed?* When I was much younger, we used to say to each other, "I dare you." Instead of looking for someone else to prod you with that challenge, you, as an adult, can dare yourself to find new courage and step forward toward your prosperity. The conditioned mind, ego, and emotions may raise their limiting points of view and say, "Watch out! You may take a wrong step." And so what if you do? You can always make a step backward or a step sideways. Is that failure? No, not really. Just another step, adjusting in the direction of your success.

"Failure" is just a label someone made up to identify an experience of not getting what they wanted when and where they wanted it. From my point of view, there really is no such thing as failure. People have rules that call one thing failure and another success. I consider each experience a success because it's an opportunity to fulfill my destiny of health, wealth, and happiness. Those experiences that don't present prosperity right away are just other sources of information, telling me what symptom I have to treat, what behavior or attitude I have to change in order to manifest the prosperity that is waiting. If you give in to something that blocks devotion (such as doubt), you can block the very energy that is supporting your success. Instead of retreating to a comfort zone that makes you feel safe but does not move you any closer to the abundance you seek, you can *use your doubt* to find out how to take the next step. The next step may be just the one that breaks you through to a level of abundance heretofore unknown.

E. Expect It to Happen

If you have put your focus and energy into the previous steps, the natural progression will be that you do expect that dream, that vision to manifest. You will expect your continued commitment because you have already accepted that your opportunities will continue to occur.

A first cousin of positive expectations is *enthusiasm,* which is the definition for tapping into divine energy. When you go inside, past your mind, emotions, and doubts, you can tap into this spiritual energy and bring it forward to improve your life. You can also share it with others and make a tangible contribution to improving the world around you. When

you learn the how-to's and become devoted to going inside (tapping into the divine energy), you will discover,
as a reality, that God is for you. When God is for you,
who can be against you? Others who have not experienced their own expanded consciousness may try to
thwart your success, but your endurance will outlast
their negativity, as long as you keep your focus positive,
on what will work for you. In fact, if you have done
steps A to E, you *have* learned to focus on what works
for you.

F. Finish It

Complete the action. Don't assume something is
completed because you are mentally, physically, or
emotionally tired. If you are washing the car and you
declare it finished when someone offers you a cool
drink, you may be deceiving yourself and aborting this
process of moving toward your own prosperity. "What?"
you might ask. "Can such a little thing as that block my
prosperity?" Many little things, added together, can
create one big block.

When you were born, you were gifted with energy,
and your life is the time span offering you the opportunity to express it any way you choose. That's your
real freedom of choice—how you choose to use your
energy. A part of you always knows the truth. It knows
whether you really finished cleaning the car. It knows
whether you really did stick to your diet. It knows
whether you did 20 push-ups or 15. It knows whether
you did one hour of meditation or spiritual exercises,
or 30 minutes, no matter what you say to yourself.

When you commit to doing something, you don't
have to give in to your "won't" power and fall short.

Instead, you can use your energy, your willpower, to complete it. When you complete things, when you tell the truth (to yourself and others), there is nothing you have to remember, no undone things or deceptions taking away your precious energy. It may be a matter of endurance, a matter of holding out to the end, despite the temptations. Do it. Get to the end. The cliché that "she or he wins who endures to the end" is accurate. In this process, the finish line is not the line ahead of you. It is the line you see as you cross it. Do you stop the second you cross it? Not necessarily. The momentum of finishing a task in devotion may propel you further than your original intentions. The result of that can be surprising rewards that are beyond your expectations.

The rewards of finishing are so much greater than the negative side, which is, to use a colloquial expression, copping out or dropping out. Instead, hold out past any fears, temptations, or frustrations. Even if you have to carry those elements while you are finishing what you committed to, *finish anyhow.* Then the next time, the fears and frustrations will not have the same weight, the same power to make the journey difficult. Next time, you can drop them earlier and enjoy the commitment until you finish it and gain the rewards.

G. Gain and Grow

If you don't gain, you can't grow. There is an immutable law of biology: grow or go. If you don't grow, you keep sliding back until you don't live. Since you are living, it makes sense to consciously choose to keep growing because that is the inherent nature of the organism called the human being. This isn't done just by affirming that you will gain and grow. It is done, once again, by acting to support that positive direction. What do you need to gain in your career? More information? Greater skills? Take those classes, read those books. Notice they are plural — not just one, but as many as it takes to equip you for success.

How will you know when you have done this enough? When your success starts manifesting. Some people may stop their growth at that point, satisfied with their initial success. That's all right, if that's all you want. But I remind you again of "grow or go." It's an eternal process on this planet and calls for you to keep on keeping on. That's the nature of one of the success formulas.

If you don't go for gaining and growing, you can always indulge in groaning. You can complain, or you can choose to go on past the complaints to the growth, getting on with what works and working it as if there were no tomorrow. By this commitment, you can gain new avenues into your creativity, which can result in a wonderful freedom. You don't have to groan when you run into obstacles. Instead, you can recognize that any obstacle can be used as a stepping-stone. You don't have to curse the obstacle, but you can find a way to use it to go higher, toward what you want. If you commit to doing just positive actions, the chances are excellent that you'll get cooperation on all levels, including the physical, emotional, mental, subconscious, and superconscious.

When you clarify a particular goal, make it manageable. Long-range goals are fine, but don't ignore the short-range goal. Why make health, wealth, and prosperity just a long-range goal? Why not also make that an immediate goal? If you are clear that you really want that, then you can support it right now. How? How about putting out that cigarette? No, don't make the *next* piece of chocolate cake the last indulgence on the way to health; make the *last* piece of chocolate cake the last. Do you get it? Start doing those things that support your goal *right now*. If you make your goal too far in the future or unreasonable (unrealistic), you may also put off doing those things that make your goal realizable and realized.

On the way to your goal, there may be some difficulties. Why? Because having a positive goal means that you have decided to gain and grow. Sometimes, as part of growth, come growing pains, but you don't have to focus on them. Like the saying goes, "Put your eye on the doughnut, not the hole."

H. Home Free

This is what we all want. Home free means that the place you go, the people you choose as your loved ones, the acts of sharing and caring, the contentment of being—these are all present.

If you try these eight steps for at least 32 consecutive days, the chances are that your life will improve considerably and you'll be on your way home.

A. Accept Your Opportunity
B. Begin to Go for It
C. Commitment
D. Devoted to Your Goal and Dream
E. Expect It to Happen
F. Finish It
G. Gain and Grow
H. Home Free

4

The Timing of Abundance, Spirit, and Precipitation

"What permits someone to move from behaviors of poverty consciousness to those of spiritual abundance and material affluence?"

Abundance, though available right now, doesn't always come in the form and timing that you wish. If you have spent many years expressing negativity that manifests as blocks (rocks) in the channel (well) into which abundance flows, then you have your work cut out for you. That's not meant to discourage you. In fact, if you're smart, you'll use that information to start doing what is necessary—right now. Instead of giving in to the part of you that may want your "goodies" right now or you "won't play," you can recognize that regardless of your wants or timelines, the balancing and the clearing will have to be done at some time, whether you like it or not. So why not like it, get to work now, and accept that the reward will come in its own timing? In approaching your life's work that way, you don't have to demand that your wants manifest immediately. In fact, this could be a good opportunity to learn to manifest patience.

In being patient, you are, once again, called upon to support yourself in the fullness of faith—faith that as you balance and clear, abundance will manifest for you in perfect timing. In the meantime, as you clear, you have the opportunity to behave toward yourself and others in the fullness of the loving Spirit within you. You may wonder how you can do that if you don't have what you want right now, but is it better to sit in your unfulfilled wants and complain? That won't do anything except create negative feelings within you. By patiently accepting what you have and don't have and by continuing to act from a positive place in the "happiness of pursuit," you'll be manifesting joy under any conditions. Joy that comes with acceptance is a special experience that you may never have known before. And in time, *in its own timing,* as long as you keep the focus and take positive action, *the abundance will come forward.* The trick is to have a good time in the meantime. The meantime does not have to be a mean time. This life is really just a journey, so you may as well enjoy the ride.

In focusing on what you want, you will be further ahead if you stay balanced. Part of balance is to recognize that the abundance that comes forward is God's abundance. As such, it is a blessing for everyone. If you think the abundance is just for you as an individual person, then we're not talking about the same abundance. You may be talking about personal greed.

Can we get abundance from greed? Yes, we can, and we also get everything that goes with it. (With the expensive sports car may come higher insurance rates. With a greedy attitude comes separation from others and, possibly, from the part of God within each of us.) When we get things through God's abundance, we also get a spiritual blessing as we share that gift. When we get something through greed, which often means causing someone else to lose, we are on our own, meaning that we may have great difficulty accessing divine guidance or support.

True manifestation includes awareness of the Divine inside you. As you grow into your divine abundance, the abundance is self-perpetuating, and you can manifest even more. The Bible says, "Let your Light so shine before men, that they may see your good works and give glory to your Father."[1] This implies that you have a connection with the Divine, which is allowing the Light to shine through you as you. In that incredible blessed energy, you can function in abundance.

As you sit in meditation, in spiritual exercises, in silence, in contemplation, you can open to the higher centers of Spirit within you, where the precipitation of abundance starts, and permit it to come down. As it does, it can present itself as intuition, in flashing pictures, forms, colors, and even words that form in the mind to start the manifestation. Sometimes you may energize them with feelings and then physically move on them. As you do that, the by-product is enthusiasm. You can ride the enthusiasm and do things that you may never have thought possible. With such enthusiasm, we have the ability to work longer hours, stay focused, and accomplish things as if they were miracles in a time warp.

Does the enthusiasm ever wane and weaken? Yes. True enthusiasm means that you are participating with an energy that comes from God. On this planet of limitations, if you don't continually reconnect to the source—Spirit—the energy can start to dissipate and possibly disappear. So it is important that you take time for yourself. For yourself, your Soul, which is part

1. Matthew 5:16 (Revised Standard Version)

of the Divine. Take time to reconnect and reawaken so Spirit can once again manifest to the mind, the emotions, the body, and right out again, riding on that enthusiasm.

At first, this may take longer than you might expect, but as you practice going within, it can happen more and more rapidly. In time, you can reconnect with the enthusiasm of Spirit as quickly as you take your next breath. You can breathe in awareness and breathe out enthusiasm. It can become as regular as your heartbeat. When you have created the habit of continually reconnecting, the Soul energy replaces the personality as the center of consciousness. The Soul will still use the mind, the emotions, and the body as vehicles through which to function, but instead of being distracted by the personality, you will be focusing from the Soul.

Many people resist going for the abundance of success, actually doing and saying things to limit themselves. Some do it because they're afraid of failure. I see people behave on the basis of, "I don't want success because I'm afraid I may fail and fall. I'd rather stay here in my limitations because, at least, I'm familiar with them." That's like a person staying in a discordant relationship with someone, arguing and fighting, but staying in it because, at least, they feel that they know the rules. But there are other choices than to go into the boxing rings of life. Rather than take comfort in any familiar limitations, why not take a wild chance and actually choose to change? I know that's sometimes difficult. It really is. Changing human behavior is something governments, psychiatrists, and authoritarian forces have tried to do, and often failed.

The only thing that changes human behavior is a human being who is not only willing to do it but courageous enough to go for it. What permits someone to move from behaviors of poverty consciousness to those of spiritual abundance and material affluence? Perhaps when someone has had an abundance of failure, when someone has become so sick and tired of being tired and sick, they may go inside and hear the voice of Spirit saying, "Life is not intended as a painful sentence. You can have joy and abundance and know it as yours."

Can prayer assist you in getting your abundance and in changing any limiting behaviors? If you pray for God to give it to you as you lie around in your bad habits, I doubt it. If, however, you pray to awaken to the power within you, if you pray for the Divine to show you the way, and if you *have the wit and courage to get up and do it,* yes, prayer can help. Once again, "Pray to God, but continue to row to shore." But row with patience. Keep rowing regardless of the weather, the waves, the temptations that may distract you. You don't have to worry about being behind schedule or making mistakes. Schedules are made by men and women, not by God. God isn't wearing the big watch in the sky. God is always present, here and now, with nowhere to go because God just is, always, in all ways.

If you don't have the idea, the answer, the information that tells you what can be done when and where, relax. Do what has to be handled in the present. Do you have to go to the bathroom? Do it now. Do you have to answer the phone? Are you hungry? Does your body need some exercise? Is there some energy that is calling you to go within and meditate? Do it. Handle the simple needs right now. You can let the process work by itself, as you handle the practical needs. The process is your having the faith that "the Spirit in me is working and will supply me with what I need when I need it."

The source of this abundance is present inside you as the vibration of Spirit. You cannot demand against it because that just won't work. Spirit does not seem to respond to demands or attempts to manipulate it. The best thing you can do, if you want to support the manifestation of abundance, is to handle what has to be done on the physical and then be quiet. Be quiet. Silence. Meditation. Calm yourself so you can receive of the divine consciousness within, which will manifest your abundance.

Imagination

In your imagination, you can visualize what you wish to take place. Be very specific and precise. Spirit is efficient. The pictures you hold in your mind are important because they manifest as thoughts that have their own energy. So be responsible to them — because you are, whether you like it or not. One important way to be responsible about what you imagine is to ask that it come forward only if it is for the highest good of all concerned.

Attunement

After imagination comes attunement. In order to attune yourself to the spiritual energies and to gain all the support from that source, you need to attune to the various levels of Spirit.

Sacred writings tell us about five lower levels, or realms, of spiritual existence: the physical, astral, causal, mental, and etheric. Each of these realms exists both within each individual and apart from the individual. Each realm corresponds to a level of expression or consciousness:

> Physical level: the physical consciousness
> Astral level: the imagination
> Causal level: the emotions
> Mental level: the mind
> Etheric level: the unconscious.

These realms exist to give each Soul the opportunity to experience all aspects, all levels, of creation. By learning each level, by completing the experience of each level, and by coming into an understanding of the "illusions" involved in each level, each of us moves closer to our goal of conscious awareness of our own Soul and becomes a co-creator under/with God.

It is an advantage to reside in the physical body because, through that vehicle, we can experience all other levels. We can experience physical, imaginative, emotional, mental, and unconscious expressions. We learn that we can create in each of these levels and that we can create in either a negative or a positive way. We can create beauty or ugliness, dreams through which we can fulfill ourselves or dreams through which we can destroy ourselves. We can create happiness or unhappiness, a bright, active, creative mind or a mind filled with the static of too many memories or unrealistic expectations of the future. We can create and maintain conscious direction over ourselves or allow the unconscious urges of our personality to control and direct us. These choices—positive and negative uses of energy—exist for each individual.

It is also stated that above the five lower realms are the positive realms of pure Spirit. The lower realms make up the negative pole of divine creation; the higher realms make up the positive pole. These are not good or bad, but are like the negative and positive poles on a battery. Both the negative pole and the positive pole are necessary for the battery to function. So, too, do the negative and positive realms together activate existence, that which we call life. Each Soul awakens to the lower realms prior to moving into co-creation with the Divinity.

In the higher realms, creation is still going on. In the lower levels, however, creation is complete—or, at least, is set in high degrees of possibility or probability. Those who prophesy do so on what they foresee as being highly probable, but these things can be changed through what has traditionally been called the grace of God. Don't let the words block you. There is the possibility that you can, by learning how to enter into the consciousness of grace, change those life patterns that have been established as probable for you.

As a person graces God (by their good works), it is possible for them to receive grace and change their pattern from one of poverty consciousness to one of abundance and prosperity.

I have looked ahead at some of the things that have been coming my way and realized that I could, through this consciousness of grace that is given to humankind by the Holy Spirit, precipitate a re-creation into this physical reality, which looks complete. The joy is unfathomable to think that although it's generally complete, through the Holy Spirit or the Divine, through moving myself into that consciousness, I can precipitate new patterns on top of the "possible" or "probable" things and completely change the old prophetic pattern.

It is also possible for you to move into this type of action. When you do, you are confronting and overcoming all conditions set up by your past actions, and you are creating in a divine consciousness throughout all universes wherein you can travel.

These actions take place through the power of grace, which is like the Divinity saying, "You may do this because you and I are one and you are working as a representative of Me. In that action where you represent Me, all must come under your dominion. All principalities, all laws, all forms of nature are now yours to command, if you so desire to command. If you wish it into being, it will be done. If you desire it, it will manifest. Before you even need it, it will be there." But notice that the beginning of this theoretical expression of Divinity says *"you and I are one."* That is the foundation upon which grace stands, and it is you who have the opportunity to establish that foundation by your choices and your actions.

I know this is accurate because I thoroughly check ideas; I work with each one before I mention it as something that will work. I go to great extremes to make sure that these things will work. I even go against the grain of a creation to see if it really will work before I present it as a workable truth, not just a hypothesis. It may be a theory to you if you can't see it yet, but as soon as you see it and *work* with it, then it can manifest for you. For example, it may sometimes be hard for you to scientifically convey your emotional experiences so that somebody else can objectively know what you mean. Yet you may start talking about your experiences, and someone else will say, "Yes, right, I understand that." This tells you that people can know things beyond what can be scientifically explained. There is a common factor within us that recognizes many of the experiences of another.

Precipitation

The ability to recreate, to change probable patterns, we call precipitation. It is the ability to precipitate into a physical reality those desirable commodities that you create on a level higher than the physical. When Moses was leading through the wilderness what was known at that time as the "chosen people," he precipitated manna from heaven to sustain them. He was able to tune in to the focal point of precipitation and bring forward sustenance through the energy patterns of the Spirit. Moses reestablished a whole new creation for the people around him when it appeared that there was nothing but a "wilderness."

As we come forward in time, there was Jesus, who was a great door opener. Whether or not you are a Christian and whether or not you believe in Jesus as the Son of God, he did open a door for humankind to walk through. He demonstrated many abilities, including precipitation. He took some loaves of bread and some fish and precipitated more of those same things; he brought through more, called it forth, and fed the multitudes. Can you imagine the ability level he was tapping? Imagine the ability Moses tapped into with all of his phenomena. He really made things appear. Many masters have tapped into this same ability and are able to precipitate and materialize objects for people.

We can take this ability of precipitation and use it in many practical ways and in many areas of our lives. We probably won't immediately develop the mastership that some Indian masters or Jesus or Moses demonstrated, but we can begin working with the ability and learn to become more masterful with it. Part of that mastery is getting the personality attuned to what is really going on, getting our minds, emotions, and bodies in line with what is. What *is*—not what we'd like it to be. In that alignment, we can receive spiritual support for completion and, thus, for the resulting manifestation of abundance.

Energy, when used to complete something, is then available as a new source for your success, for you have gained the rewards of proper attunement on all levels. When you have this attunement, there is an irresistible energy that can affect others' subconscious. People may feel this energy and be attracted to you, drawn to your attunement, because you are in harmony with your environment. This gives you the ability to work with authority and to work as an authority. This is not a dictatorial authority, but an authority gained through knowledge, experience, and patience, an authority in terms of handling responsibility and fulfilling commitments. People who are successful in handling authority have demonstrated the ability to do what has to be done at the time and to take appropriate action.

With appropriate identification, imagination, attunement, and action, you are declaring what is to be manifested as your abundance. And it will come in the most effective way, which is for your highest good. You may have been programming for a Porsche, for example, but somehow the funds came through for a less expensive American car. How come? Perhaps the spiritual forces aligned themselves with your attunement, creating conditions where you wouldn't have a car that would tempt you to drive erratically at high speeds, endangering your and other people's lives.

Can Spirit work that specifically? When you are in attunement, yes. Spirit can work in such a way as to have someone driving exceedingly slowly in front of you. Instead of getting impatient and blowing the horn, imagine that Spirit may have sent that person to slow you down so you would avoid a drastic accident just ahead.

You can attune yourself to the spiritual levels by going within. A by-product of that is accessing divine protection and manifesting abundance for yourself, in areas ranging from traffic to health, wealth, and spiritual inner awareness. That kind of attunement is, indeed, for the highest good.

This abundance, however, is not to be hoarded, lest it dissipate and the joy it can bring disappear. There is an apt expression: "From the one to whom much is given, much is expected." Once you have been shown the laws of manifestation, it is expected that you will then manifest abundance for and with others. As you include others, your abundance can manifest to an even greater level. Instead of thinking in terms of "me," you relate to "us" in your family and your immediate community, which allows fellowship to go where Spirit directs it, while, at the same time, you responsibly handle this physical level.

It has been said, "You are all gods. You are all abundant. You are all creators." As you know this and experience the joy of being part of this, you can experience the ease of creating abundance, sharing it, and creating even greater abundance, as an ongoing, replenishing process, all in the perfect timing of Spirit.

5

Finding the Hidden Treasures

"Prosperity, in terms of true value, has to enrich the human beings involved."

When prosperity is mentioned, most people immediately think of material prosperity. Translated to specifics, it might be a house with a manageable mortgage, a fully paid-for car, and enough money in the bank not to worry about having enough money in the bank.

When I talk about prosperity, however, the material area is secondary. What good are all the goodies if you don't have the capacity to enjoy them? If your inner life is filled with anguish and anxiety, all the outer accoutrements do not add up to a life of prosperity. In order to truly enjoy physical luxury and comfort, you need to have the capacity for joy within you.

I have been in theaters, movies, and concerts where a comedian will do a routine, and many people will laugh uproariously. Simultaneously, others may sit there in stony silence, laughter dormant within them. Even though they paid the same price for tickets, they might be bored while others are totally entertained. Sometimes, of course, this is a matter of personal taste in humor, and at other times it is a matter of the accessibility of inner joy. If you have strong feelings of guilt or upset and you go to hear a comedian, laughter may be hard to come by if you are unable to let those feelings go. If you are being run by your emotions, you may also limit your capacity to enjoy your outer prosperity. Inner prosperity will not necessarily produce material abundance, but it sure is necessary if you are to enjoy it.

Material abundance may also be more accessible if you are internally balanced. Part of this balance involves being at one with what is going on in the present. This does not necessarily mean liking it or even preferring it, but accepting it without judgment. If you have a cold, you can curse the elements, blame the weather, and be very upset, but how does that help you or the cold? Another choice is to accept that you have a cold, do what is best under those conditions, and even enjoy it. How can you enjoy a cold? Well, instead of feeling resistant, angry, or upset, you might relax, rest, enjoy the respite from your normally busy workday, drink lots of fluids, watch a TV show or read a book, and generally just lie back and give your body time to recover. A cold can be your body's way of telling you that you need some more rest. Since you have little choice, why not enjoy the rest?

Cooperating with what is going on contributes to oneness—a balance and an inner tranquility that are the essence of true abundance. If you go for materiality with an attitude of tranquility (not greed), when you get it, you will probably have the capacity to enjoy it without being hooked by it.

When people get a material thing they have been yearning for, they sometimes become addicted to it. For example, I know a man who—after many years—finally got an expensive foreign car. I mean, it was *very* expensive. When he drove it, he was concerned that other cars on the road would not get too close, so sometimes he drove too fast and other times, too slow. When he drove into the parking lot of a store, he often became concerned that people might park their cars too near his and and scratch it when they opened their car doors. His life became one of major concern about the well-being of his car, all at the expense of the well-being of himself.

Then, while he was attending a consciousness-raising workshop, his car was stolen. When he realized this, he panicked, even though he was fully insured. By the time the police came, something happened to my friend. Instead of complaining and being upset, he broke out laughing. The police couldn't understand his laughter in the face of having his expensive car stolen. He laughed because he finally realized that — for him — it wasn't a matter of his car being stolen; it was a matter of his being released, freed from his obsession. He recognized that he had been a slave to his car, instead of his car having served him. Now that it was gone, he was free and had back all that "car-energy" to use as he wished. He was, once again, whole.

To be whole means to have the choice of how we use our energy. Our energy is, perhaps, the most valuable thing that we have dominion over. We have just so much energy. It's as if we're born with a certain quotient, and how we use it is part of our freedom of choice. I expect that when we express in anger, greed, and lust, we expend enormous amounts of this energy. When we express loving care and consideration, I expect that our energy gets replenished, like getting interest from a savings account.

When I encourage people to bypass the temptations of greed, I am not doing this from a moralistic position. Rather, I am being practical. If greed produced real joy, I probably wouldn't suggest moving beyond it. But greed corrupts and erodes our gift of energy. It limits our opportunity to enjoy the fruits of our efforts.

Prosperity, in terms of true value, has to enrich the human beings involved. If you buy something from someone, an opportunity exists for each of you to be enriched through a fair deal. As a result, both of you — human beings each — can come away from the transaction with an experience of increased worth — not just on the material level, but on the human-exchange level. Although prices may fluctuate, the human being is priceless. There may be things on this planet that are enormously expensive and luxurious, and they are of little true value if you don't connect to the inner treasures.

These inner treasures are described by some as the true self or essence; by others, as the hidden treasures. The treasures are hidden, yet they are available. We find treasures in the *personality*, which includes our thinking, the *emotions*, the *body*, and *how we put it all together and express it in the world.*

When we indulge in greed or negative thinking, we can corrupt part of our treasure. But if we look at someone else not as a competitor, but as another human being with whom we can negotiate so that each of us can have an experience of respect and reasonable profit, our treasure doesn't have to be depleted. In fact, the treasure can increase through acts of caring and consideration for others. Scriptures of all different religious groups tell us that as we think in our heart, thus we become.

Thinking in our heart is connecting an emotional, loving quality to the content of the mind. Otherwise, thinking can be limited to an intellectual experience. Intellect without caring can be cold and sterile, not exactly an abundant experience. Conversely, if we have only emotions, we may not be accessing our wisdom. Thinking in our heart includes the ability to see into what is present and to put it together in a chain of thoughts that we can move on physically as we share with other people.

It is important that we purify our thinking because our thoughts lead us in this world. It's like my friend with the expensive car: If his thoughts had been that the car was an inanimate object that was to serve him and, in time, would rust and get scratched, then he would have been much freer to have enjoyed the car. It was his attitude that made it a limiting experience, not a fact of reality.

The hidden treasures are also located in another place: They are concealed under time. Out of a small acorn the mighty oak does grow — in time. At one time, the Grand Canyon was a little gully. At one time, you and I were infants crawling around in wet diapers. How we grow, or how we resist growth, is up to us. Time goes on regardless of our level of cooperation. Time, otherwise known as life, has a way of bringing forward the lessons we have to learn. Whether we learn things the hard or the easy way is up to each of us. So is the length of time we take to learn.

In this lifetime, there are treasures awaiting your discovery. You may sometimes be unwilling to put in the effort to uncover the treasures, thinking that you can wait for later because it takes too much effort to claim them. It might help if you realized that you are in your "laters" now. Why put off discovering the treasures that are within you? You don't have to be a victim of time. You can get going right now and use time as an ally instead of an obstacle.

Of course, some people will not go for the "straight and narrow" and, as a result of not taking care of business on all levels, may get into difficulty, into trouble. The interesting thing is that even for those who go that route, treasures are also hidden in troubles. There is an old spiritual song that goes, "Nobody knows the trouble I've seen." When you are down and out and there is no place else to go—so low that you can't go any further down, and even the gutter looks like up to you—then you have the opportunity to try something that you may have been avoiding. It might be going for the truth of who you really are. This doesn't have to be a revelation or a ritual, just a moment of connecting to the essence within you (regardless of what you call it), with no cover or protective act, just saying the truth. It might simply be, "Help." If you say that, asking for assistance with no strings attached, if your heart is in that word, you just might get the help you ask for. Remember, however, that the help may often come in different forms than those you might have expected. I doubt if you'll get rent money falling like manna from heaven, but you may get an insight into how to get a better-paying job. You may not immediately get that mate you'd like, but you might get clarity about how to improve your relationships.

It is up to you to accept the help and put it into action. You need to take the information offered, weigh the possibilities and the choices, and then start doing. Many people have had great ideas that they've written down and then did nothing about them. Years later, one of those ideas may have become a hugely successful product because someone else did something with the same idea. The person may say, "I had the idea first!" So what? You can have a marvelous idea, and unless you move on it, it remains just a marvelous idea. Then, in its demise through neglect, it may take energy from you because you know, way down deep, that if you had given it your best shot and acted on it, it might have worked.

It's a matter of taking action to support your goal. This may mean making that phone call that's difficult for you, but doing it anyway. It may mean studying for an exam, practicing or rehearsing for greater periods of time, or spending less and saving more so you can get the training you need for success. Regardless of the difficulties or troubles presented to you, if you have the will to persist, you are likely to uncover the treasures hidden within the folds of difficulties and challenges. He or she wins who endures to the end.

In other words, as you endure, you eventually have to awaken to other sources where the treasures are hidden: self-improvement. The inner self, the true self, does not need improvement, but the personality-self may very well need improvement in order for you to achieve the success for which you yearn. On the one hand, if I offered you a million dollars, would you be willing to change? Most of you would say yes. On the other hand, if I told you that you don't know when and how you'll get the money, but you need to start changing right now, some of you might resist.

There are no guarantees, particularly in terms of time lines and rewards, but if you are going to get what you want, you may as well face it—there are dues to be paid. Those dues do not have to be painful. Again, it depends on your attitude. If you dig in with your ego and refuse to change, then you may also be sinking yourself into a rut of resistance. Success rides high and may miss you below it. A great part of self-improvement is a willingness to change. A great part of change is letting go.

Let go of anything that is in between you and your success. It could be aspects of your personality. For example, you may laugh too much or smile too little. You may talk too much and listen too little. You may want approval in a form that is uncomfortable for others. Or your personality may be well-balanced, and it may be a matter of letting go of weight, alcohol, tobacco, fried foods, sugar products, or even poor work-habits. When you let go of something limiting you, you are making room for unlimited abundance and prosperity to pour through.

Can we have inner peace and connection with our hidden treasures and still maintain a balance of abundance in this physical world? Yes—and it isn't always easy. Even with all the hidden treasures becoming available to you, in order for you to have material things, you may still have to go into the world, strive, and labor. The trick is to remember to keep going in and out. That is the key: Go in and connect to that place where everything is full, content, and peaceful; then, with that joy, go out and share your loving consideration, wisdom, and balance.

6

Tithing to the Source

"Our job is to become aware of our divine inheritance and lay claim to it by overcoming our lower nature so we can live in the awareness of our Soul."

One of the fundamental errors that we have as human beings is greed, which is manifested mostly in terms of money or monetary value. Greed, by its very nature, is a striking against the riches within oneself because it appears that there is never enough here in the world. Our eyes are always hungry.

We can help to break the greed pattern by tithing, giving 10 percent of our personal wealth. When a person tithes, two levels are activated — a level here in this world and, at the same time, a mystical, invisible level. The mystical is a communication saying, "You are abundant and handle abundance well, so here's some more." The other level, in this world, is when we look at our abundance and contribute joyfully through tithing. We are actually cheerful about it. This action sets up a countenance that is a form of glory in the human being, and that glory attracts more abundance.

When one person becomes free of materiality, it's like an infection going the other way. Instead of greed affecting honest people, honest people start affecting the greedy.

When Abram (later Abraham) was traveling home with the riches of battle after warring with a nearby king, he was met by Melchizedek. "Then

Melchizedek king of Salem brought out bread and
wine. He was priest of God Most High, and he blessed
Abram. . . . Then Abram gave him a tenth of
everything."[1] As soon as Abram saw Melchizedek, the
wisdom of Abram's heart knew he was seeing one who
was with God. He knew that he was to give back 10 percent of all he had in the world to the representative of
God, and so reinforced the law of tithing. A spiritual
covenant was set up, whereby humankind is to give a
tenth of its increase (what a person receives that is his
or hers) back to God (or to their source of spiritual
teachings).

As humankind fulfills its part of the covenant by
giving 10 percent to God, then God fulfills its part by
continually blessing us. Our job is to become aware of
our divine inheritance and lay claim to it by overcoming our lower nature so we can live in the awareness of
our Soul. When we tithe to the church or to the source
of our spiritual teachings, as representatives of the
Divinity, we are making the material world let go of us.
So tithing, part of a spiritual law, assists us in getting
free of materialistic confinement.

You tithe also to perpetuate the good news. You
give to your church, synagogue, mosque, or group as if
you are giving to yourself. In fact, when people give to
the source of their spiritual teachings, they are really
just giving to themselves in another form. Your tithe
brings greater and greater solidarity to the group.
More than that, you give as a way of supporting your
own spiritual unfoldment and awakening. You are
learning how to focus your energy, how to concentrate
your energy, and how to reveal your energy.

1. Genesis 14:18-20 (New International Version)

How do we give when we give? With a condition? No. When we give a dollar to someone, we let it go. When we let go, the other person can do anything with it they want. That's tithing—when you are able to take of the "sweat of your brow," translate it into value (i.e., money), and then give out of gratitude.

In biblical times, people who tithed often received a hundredfold more than what they had given. (When they received their hundredfold, they then tithed by giving 10 percent of that.) If you tithe for a reward, however, you are not doing it for the proper reason. You give as a recognition of appreciation. Actually, the tithe doesn't belong to you in the first place. You are just restoring it to its rightful owner, God. You open yourself to the flow of abundance by saying, "I'm tithing, and now, God, I am open to receive whatever you reward me with that I am in need of, even though I may not even know what it is." It might be good health, it might be that a child is born, it might be that somebody pays a debt that is due you. It might be that your spouse's sickness is cleared up. You need to be open to receive. The giving *and* the receiving are both part of the process of tithing.

Some people say, "I can't afford to tithe." It might be more appropriate if they said, "I can't afford *not* to tithe." It's like having a water pump. You may start the pump, and no water comes out. But if you pour a little water down the pump and then start to pump, water comes out. Tithing is like priming the pump. Of course, the unknown question is, "How much water do you pour down there before you get some out?" And the answer is, "You pour until the water comes out." In other words, you keep tithing with the knowledge that the blessings are present and will come to you in God's perfect timing.

To people who say, "I'm broke," I say, "Send a dime." One person in a discussion of tithing said, "This is my last quarter," and he gave that to his church. It was also his bus money home. Someone saw him do that and said, "Can I give you a lift home?" The person took him home and, on the way, hired him and gave him an advance of $100. He went to work the next day, and those two have worked as partners ever since. This man said to me, "Who'd believe it? I gave away my last quarter." I said, "Who cares who believes it!" He said, "You ought to tell people about it." So I do.

Historically, people have tended to trust in materiality for their success. Instead of trusting in the source of their abundance for their success, they trust in money or riches. Then they stop tithing so they can have a lot more materiality they can trust. It usually isn't too long until something of a negative nature happens to them. Why? Some say coincidence, and others say it's because they have forsaken the Lord. It is said that if you break an agreement, you, in that act, have "given up" the Lord. Can that be corrected? Of course. Any mistake can be corrected, and you can always "get yourself right" with God. It's just a matter of right thinking and right doing. Right thinking is recognizing, as Abram did, that all things come from Divinity. Right doing is tithing to the source of your spiritual teachings, thus restoring the law of tithing as an ongoing action in your life so your life can open up for things to flourish again.

It's important to tithe with love in your heart. It's not enough to just give 10 percent. It needs to be done with loving, caring, and sharing, the same way you would care for your own family, for the people dearest to you. There is something beyond the giving of the 10 percent, and this is called being a joyful giver. You automatically give joyfully when you love the Lord with all your body, mind, and Soul. This is learning to put God first in your life. If all you can give is two dollars, and that two dollars is all that you have, and if you give it lovingly and unconditionally, it may be more than the 10 percent given by those who have much and don't give with a joyful attitude.

One of the hardest addictions on the planet to break is possessiveness, the attitude of "I own" and "This is mine." I am not saying that outlook is wrong. I understand that when people work for something, they consider that they own it. That may be accurate on one level, but incomplete in the larger sense. On this level of human laws, we do have ownership, and that's appropriate. What I'm emphasizing is not falling into the trap of being attached to what you think you own.

Each of us needs to recognize that what we own isn't really ours because "the earth is the Lord's and the fulness thereof."[2] In relationship to what we think we own, the act of tithing is a way of saying, "I am not attached to this physical object. I am not attached to that thing called money. In tithing, I recognize that all my wealth is because I am straight with God. When I tithe, it is an expression of the Spirit within me." This attitude blesses you so that the "slings and arrows of outrageous fortune" never really touch you. They may touch your personality, mind, or emotions, but if you've invested in the spirit of who you really are, the "slings and arrows" will fall short.

2. Psalm 24:1 (Revised Standard Edition)

A friend of mine, who is healthy, happy, and very comfortable financially, has been tithing from his gross income for about 14 years. In his work, he pays an agent 10 percent of the total amount he receives, even before taxes are deducted. That's the way his business relationship with the agent works. When asked why he doesn't tithe to his church from his *net* ("Because, after all, the government takes so much!"), his response is, "Why should I give Divinity's representative less than my agent?" This man recognizes the source of his prosperity and makes sure he expresses this knowledge in many ways, one of which is tithing.

Ten percent off the top actually makes it easy. I heard a woman say, "I tithe 10 percent, and if I gave any more, I'd be so rich I couldn't stand it." She was very wealthy through her cooperation with the law of tithing.

When the tithing is done unconditionally, your reward may come in many ways, including as a flash of insight into the heart of God. You may say, "This is worth $10 million. How do I tithe on that?" The answer is that you tithe on the money that comes to you. The other comes through grace, and you can't tithe on grace; you can only have the abundance of it.

When a person commits to tithing, something inside of them works differently from that day forward. Conditions may or may not immediately change on the physical level, but inside, it can work wonders. A very common experience among tithers is that they find that the 90 percent that they have left over after tithing stretches further than the 100 percent they had before they started to tithe. Many tithers also experience a reduction in their debts. In fact, two people I know, after only two to three years of tithing, cleared themselves of debts that had been with them for over ten years. In these and other examples, it's as if the act of tithing brings a person into greater harmony and responsibility with their environment, and this, in turn, opens a place for greater abundance to come forward.

In Malachi, it is asked "Will a man rob God? Yet you rob me . . . in tithes and offerings."[3] The question is, Can God actually be robbed? No, but the covenant can be broken, and that is robbing God of the covenant. Later on in the same chapter, it is said, "Bring the whole tithe into the storehouse. . . . Test me in this . . . and see if I will not throw open the floodgates of heaven and pour out so much blessing that you will not have room enough for it."[4]

So, you may want to check it out with a joyful attitude of saying, "Lord, I am open to receive whatever it is that you bless me with." And then discover for yourself the blessings of fulfilling God's covenant.

3. Malachi 3:8 (New International Version)
4. Malachi 3:10 (New International Version)

7

Creating and Using Your Money Magnet

"Tithing to the source of your spiritual teachings and to yourself is part of the process of prosperity that is your heritage."

Have you ever wondered why misers have money? They hang on to it. We have a classic image of the miser as a little old man huddled up, holding his money close, counting his coins on the table, one after another, and checking them off on paper. A greedy person, all pinched in. I'm sure this image doesn't fit many of the people who have a tremendous amount of money, but we can still ask, Why do some people pull money to themselves while others don't? There is a theory that if you took all of the money in the world and distributed it equally, in ten years you would find the money grouped again in the hands of a few people. They would have or control most of the money. Why would this happen? Luck? No. It's because these people focus their awareness, most of the time, on money. I encourage focusing attention on spiritual things to get to Spirit; they often focus on money as a kind of god, and they pull it to themselves. Is it possible to experience spiritual abundance and financial abundance simultaneously? Yes.

Let's look at the Bible as a reference point. Jesus said that "the kingdom of God is within you."[1] There is another law in which we take a certain percentage of our money and give to the God within us. An ancient mystical society called this the Law of Amra, which is giving to yourself.

We give back a portion of what we make to God, as a form of humility and as a way of acknowledging God as the source of our supply. If God's kingdom is within us, then that's where God is residing within a consciousness—not as a total being, but as an essence. If this is true, you should be paying 10 percent to yourself. You work hard for your money, very hard. Then, when payday comes, you may pay everyone else first. You pay your taxes and your bills, and if there is anything left over, you get it. Yet 10 percent of that should go to God first—not 10 percent of what is left over, but the *first* 10 percent of that which you receive.

When you give to yourself (after you have tithed to the source of your spiritual teachings), you then take 10 percent of your check and pay yourself first—in cash. Don't write a check because that is a symbol, and you have to have the actual cash. Paying yourself is paying to the God within, and this takes care of the spiritual. You can still give money to the church, but keep it separate: "This is the church fund, this is the car fund, this is for food, this is the rent, this is the clothing fund, but first this is the fund that goes to me." You pay yourself before you pay the other bills.

You might ask why you can't write a check like you do for everybody else and just know that you are going to get paid first. It doesn't work that way. Like attracts

1. Luke 17:21 (King James Version)

like. Money attracts money. There's an old saying, "The poor get poorer, and the rich get richer." Why do banks attract more money? It's almost as if they have a magnet there because money *is* a magnet. You can establish your own money magnet by tithing to yourself, in cash, every time you receive money, whether it's a paycheck, a bonus, or a gift. Tithing to the source of your spiritual teachings and to yourself is part of the process of prosperity that is your heritage.

To understand how this works, let's look at how the subconscious mind (or the basic self or lower self) perceives money. In comes the paycheck, and the subconscious mind sees you (the conscious self) getting this money and tithing 10 percent of the gross to the spiritual organization of your choice and also putting aside an additional 10 percent into your own private money magnet. In tithing, you recognize that all things come from God, and the money magnet contribution is a reward for yourself. The subconscious thinks, "That 10 percent is for me! You mean I'm going to get something? You are really going to pay me now? Me! Mine! I'm going to bring more in; I'll open my consciousness!" You can be walking down the street, and there will be a five dollar bill. The subconscious will say, "Get that five dollar bill! I get 10 percent of that; that's 50 cents. You can do whatever you want with the rest, but 50 cents goes to me."

You have to make your subconscious feel worthwhile by keeping your agreements. You may have betrayed it before by saying you'd do something and then going back on that. Then it may say, "You've promised me a lot of things but have given me nothing." It takes a concerted effort to reverse these feelings of betrayal. When you keep a money magnet—always putting 10 percent of what you get into the money magnet, in cash—the subconscious mind will learn that it can trust you. It can trust that it will get its portion, its 10 percent, and so will work diligently to bring in money to you.

Keep the money magnet where you can actually touch it. If you put that money into the bank, the *bank* gets your money magnet. As far as the subconscious mind is concerned, putting the money into the bank takes it away. You have to be able to go to that money and pick it up and hold it or count it. You keep 10 percent at home, and it will pull more money to it. Once you have your money magnet going, don't use it for any other purpose. Don't spend it. It is a magnet; if you spend it, you have lost your magnet. Don't borrow from your money magnet; if you borrow from it, it's gone. Put 10 percent in the magnet. This is important. Don't put in 11 or 12 percent, and don't put in 9 percent. Put in 10 percent; there's something "magical" about it.

Use your remaining money for other areas and other funds. You might want to have a fund set aside for your wants—not for what you need, but for what you want. It might not be a big fund at first, and you might have to limit your wants quite a bit. But as your money magnet pulls in more, your "want fund" may also grow.

When you start, your money magnet may be very small. Just keep putting 10 percent in there. Pretty soon, you will have a thousand dollars. It starts pulling rather rapidly then, and your other funds—your want fund, your food fund, your fun fund, your car fund, your clothing fund, and so on—start building rather rapidly, too, and they may start building up more than you thought possible. In the meantime, the money magnet fund also keeps growing, and you can look in there and think, "Oh, look at all that money." It's not a greedy consciousness because you're not trying to take the money with you, but while you're here, you'll have the pressure of the environment lifted.

If you are a homemaker who doesn't have outside work, you might start a money magnet with the money that you have put aside for household items, the money you use to take care of the home. That's your "salary," and you put 10 percent of that into a money magnet. Your husband may say, "Honey, 10 percent of my overall check is the money magnet"; then the money that you use for the house should go for expenditures and not into a money magnet. But if he doesn't do this, then you can take 10 percent of what he gives you and start a money magnet.

You need to have an understanding with your partner about how you're going to handle this. If both the husband and wife work, they can create a money magnet together. They can both put their money in together and say, "That's more me." His subconscious is saying, "That's mine," and her subconscious is saying, "That's mine," and they will both be building.

After you have put the money in your money magnet, get it out periodically and count it. A lot of people sleep with it under their beds, in their pillows, by them. Do you know why some people collect coins? Do you know what they are always doing with their coin collections? They are always looking at them and admiring how beautiful the coins are. They can say, "I really have a rare one. It is brilliant, uncirculated. And look at the date on it. They have made a mistake on this one." This type of attention, this type of focus, pulls more coins to them.

What do you do when you get ten thousand dollars in your money magnet? That ten thousand dollars will pull in more money than a thousand dollars will pull in. What if you need that money in some other area of your life? You *won't* need it because the money magnet will pull more money to you. All you have to do is keep putting 10 percent in there and use the other 90 percent in other areas.

There is one catch here. You may think, "With all that money, I'll load myself down with responsibilities. I'll buy a house here and a house at the beach and a house in the mountains. And that means I am going to have three different roofs, three sets of plumbing, three gas bills, etc. Do I really want that?" The money isn't there for you to load yourself down. It's there so you'll get what you really need. A key is to keep your need here in the present.

Most people desire fantastic things: the best clothing, food, cars, houses, and so on. You can eat the best food and end up with gout or stomach trouble, or you can just eat to fulfill your need (nutrition). You can live in a house that fulfills the needs of what you are accomplishing. Anything else that you get is a gift, and perhaps you should give deep thanks for that. Deep thanks can be sharing this consciousness of creation with other people to help them lift.

You can't enter into this consciousness by saying, "All right, I'm broke and I'm going to magnetize myself for a hundred dollars. I need it tomorrow, which is Saturday. This will be interesting; I'll just see what happens." Nothing happens, and you say, "I didn't think it would work." That's right. There's no need to watch and place an expectation when it can't possibly take place. It *can* take place through the money magnet.

As you get more money, if you aren't careful, there can come the fear of losing it, and that fear can be difficult to work with. If the money is yours, you can't lose it, and if it is not yours, it's going to go — one way or another — so there's really no need to be fearful. It is a good idea, of course, to keep your money magnet in a safe place in your home, and if it makes you feel better, you can split it up and put it in different places in the house. The important thing is to be careful not to institute a fear pattern. If you do, you may not be working with money as a spiritualized medium of exchange (used for upliftment); instead, you may be in a consciousness of hoarding. Nobody can take "spiritualized" money. They simply can't take it. That is yours.

A money magnet is to be recognized and relished in its physicality. You could also invest it in something like real estate, where you can walk on the property and know it is yours. This is different from putting it into the bank. With property, you can physically be there and say, "This ten-thousand-dollar lot is mine." It will start pulling in more of the same. If you buy a house or land to build upon, you can be there on it and know, "This is mine to do my work." But if you buy a boat to ride around in, you have to think, "Is this to do my work?" If it's not, then use your "fun fund" to buy your boat, but don't use your money magnet.

Don't put all your money magnet into one area.
You might invest in such things as a mutual fund,
bonds, or a savings account. I am not a financial ad-
visor, so don't use this advice from that point of view.
My emphasis is that if you get dividends from these,
put 10 percent of those dividends back into your money
magnet. I don't suggest playing the stock market with
money magnet funds because that involves an element
of chance, but, if necessary, investing in a reasonably
secure, low-risk mutual fund might be an appropriate
use of money magnet funds. If you do this, remember
to keep the certificates of any investment where you
can get to them and review them physically.

Most rich people have a vault or safe in their
house, and they keep jewels, stock certificates, bonds,
and money there. Stop and think about this for a few
minutes, and you'll know this whole thing makes sense.
They are smart enough to know that thieves have a
money consciousness, too. The theme of the movie *To
Catch a Thief* is that you need a thief to catch a thief.
If you can put the money there, an unscrupulous person with a consciousness of money can also tune in to it.
A thief who is adept at this can walk right in, pick it
up, walk out, and leave everything else alone. Somebody says, "Inside job." It sure was: The inner
awareness was there. Some who are concerned about
this open a safety deposit box in a bank and visit it fre-
quently, not only to put in jewelry, certificates, and
money but to actually count them.

You can invest money from your money magnet as
long as you can keep it within your grasp, keep it close
to you. And you also need to look at the reason it's being invested in these areas. Are you doing this out of

fear that somebody's going to steal it, which could be a motivation from poverty consciousness, or are you going into it to multiply it, which is seeing money as a spiritualized medium of exchange? For example, you can buy land and walk on it and know that it has the potential to grow in worth. There are a lot of ways to handle this, but if you do it out of fear, you may lose. It's harder to work with the Divine in fear patterns. If you create fear, that which you fear may come upon you. You set the patterns in motion and then say, "It didn't work." We say, "It worked all right, but not the way you wanted."

If you are investing your money magnet out of fear, it might be more valuable for you to actually keep the money — rather than invest it — because that is your magnet. A number of people have accumulated a lot of money and invested in a house or a business and gone broke because their magnet was gone. Many business people will tell you to keep about 30 thousand dollars in reserve if you are going into business. They often think it's there in case you have a bad time. Maybe; it's also your magnet. If you understand this, you are going to have some doors open to you quickly, and you won't have to be a miser about it. You'll use your common sense in using these forces to pull wealth to you. A nice thing about this is that not one of you will go up the financial scale alone; you're going to take at least a half-dozen people with you because that is also the law of spiritual attraction.

The consciousness of many people, when they start in spiritual or metaphysical work, is to use the spiritual energy to get money rather than to grow spiritually. When you grow spiritually, however, you learn how to handle the money through a spiritual consciousness, and you can become so wealthy that you almost can't believe it. Once you know how to handle it, once you step into the spiritual and acquire money spiritually, it can't be taken from you.

It can be hard to be spiritual when you are worried about feeding the children and putting shoes on their feet. It's hard because you are worried and concerned about the physical; you are locking into the physical element. As long as you have one bill you can't pay, just one, that's the one you are probably going to worry about: They might attach your paycheck, or they might come after you. That's the one you dread, and when you dread it, it controls you. When you are controlled, it's harder to do your spiritual work. You have to be free in order to receive your spiritual gifts, and that means no attachment, no desires. You have the money there to be used whenever it's appropriate. If you don't need the money, you are free.

When we learn how to handle money in this way, we are really, in the larger sense, learning to focus our attention by bringing money forward. Humans seem to have an inclination to accumulate money, and when we have learned to do this, we can then focus our attention on other things to bring them into existence. Money is like a practice round.

What we are talking about is the idea of precipitation. The money magnet will pull money to you. Even more than that, you can also learn how to precipitate into your beingness those qualities that can enhance your life. The money magnet is like lifting weights. It's getting you in shape to reach into the greater things and work within the higher levels. It's a process of training the mind, training the consciousness, learning to place the desires and emotions where you want them. It is tuning in to those qualities you want and bringing them forward. Then you find out that you are able to tune in to an even greater frequency than the money magnet frequency. You'll tune in to divine grace and manifest everything you need for yourself. You will learn to precipitate your happiness and your joy because you will tune in to it through your own joy within.

Once we — and this means everyone — can reach in and stir our spiritual inner awareness a little bit, so many doors can open. Stirring this inner awareness is like my saying, "I want you to start a money magnet; here is a hundred dollars to start it," and the money starts coming to you. This is an awakening into what some call the Light, a universal energy and power into which we can all tap.

Because the earth's polarity is negative, the primary force of energy on the planet is negative. But the Light, the force of energy that comes from the higher realms of existence, is positive. By learning to attune your consciousness to that, you can bring the Light into your life and, using the positive energy, pull positive things to yourself.

The Light may seem a little intangible to you for a time. Even if you are unable to see it, however, you may be able to see what it can do in your life, how it can change and lift. Even when you are not aware of it, it's lifting you. In fact, it's the energy that sustains you.

As you attune your consciousness to the Light, as you focus on the positive, you will bring more of the positive to you. You will also find that this energy works both ways. If you want hatred and bigotry, tune to it, my friends, and you can have it. If you want unhappiness, go ahead — be unhappy. Tune in to it, hold it to you, and you can have it. But if you want joy, love, harmony, well-being, and upliftment, tune in to that; create that. The law of precipitation doesn't care. It will provide for you either way. No matter what you ask for, you may very well get it. That's why we say, "Be careful what you ask for," because it's likely to come to you.

You may sometimes say, "I understand this, and I've really been tuning to the Light and positive energy. So why aren't things the way I want them? Why am I down here and not up there?" And I'll ask, "Did you hold to that Light action all the time?" You may say, "Well, no. A couple of times, I just gave up on everything and got depressed and down and called a few people names. When I went to the market, the woman in front of me stole my parking place, and I wanted to hit her with my car." And I'll answer, "You have to take care of those thoughts and feelings and actions when they come back to you. You've been busy creating *that* instead of joy and happiness and love and sharing." Those things that you create are returned to you. So if you're smart, you'll create balance and harmony and love. Then you can receive that.

The longer, the more intently you can hold your focus on a point, the sooner you can precipitate that point into greater manifestation for yourself. *If you want love, be love.* When you are manifesting love, however, people may want to put you down and harm you because they are unable to handle the loving and may think you are vulnerable to hurt. They may want to and try to, but their negative efforts do not have to have a negative effect on you. I know that it can be a challenge at these times to hold the positive focus and to continue to put out love, no matter what. This doesn't mean you have to be a fool and let people walk all over you and take advantage of you—not at all. It does mean that you do not return anger with anger, hurt with another hurt, or a name with another name. You break the cycle of negativity and replace it with the positive action, which can be just as active, just as dynamic, as the negativity.

The forces of negativity (I call them the "loyal forces of the opposition") are just as loyal to the action they represent as those of the Light are to the action they represent. The negative forces will do everything possible to knock down your positive position. It can certainly be a challenge, but if you can hold the positive position and use only the positive energy to activate your life, the negative forces will not be able to harm or hurt you in any way. It will simply not be possible.

Humankind is walking in a great dispensation right now. There are greater amounts of positive energy being precipitated down to the planet than ever before, and more people are becoming aware of it and are being given the opportunity to choose consciously between the negative and positive forces. When the Light comes into any area, it will throw up the negative elements to clear them away. In many ways, that's what is happening on the planet today. The Light is coming in more strongly and is throwing up the negativity so it can be cleared away. It is not necessarily a negative action, although it may certainly appear that way sometimes. It can be very positive, however, because it is clearing away the old negative patterns and making way for the positive patterns now coming forward.

As you move into the positive actions, as you learn to build a money magnet to bring you greater wealth, a happiness magnet to bring you greater happiness, and a health magnet to bring you greater health, you may find that you want to share your knowledge and abilities with others, to become of greater service. Become a positive precipitator first because until you can really work these ideas, it will probably be difficult to share them with others.

You may sometimes feel a great love or compassion for people but, at the same time, you may not be able to share because sharing it with them may betray their consciousness or give them the wrong impression of the nature of your feelings. With this realization, you begin to move into the concept that we call working "for the highest good of all concerned."

When you do work for the highest good, you will be very careful not to betray, misrepresent, hurt, or upset anyone. It is for these reasons that many times, when people ask me questions, I don't answer. And they may feel that I don't like them. Often, my not answering shows that I must work for the highest good and on the highest level for that person as well as for myself. When you enter into this quality, you may find a difficulty in sharing this great, everlasting love, and that may become your loneliness. You may feel bottled up in a great world of love and joy, and you really can't let it out, except through the action that loves and supports unconditionally, the action that sees the positive in every event and uses every experience as a tool for learning, as a stepping-stone, not a stumbling block.

You don't need to despair and get discouraged if things don't always seem to go your way. The situations of this world are teaching devices. If you feel desperate, this may make you focus and direct yourself. If you are discouraged, this can make you say, "Why is this going on?" Then you may start searching and precipitating down the answers. Your answers are already within you, and if you would sit down quietly for 20 or 30 minutes, you could have your answers.

If you look to someone else to provide you with all the answers, why are you needed? You may have to search a little bit and, perhaps, have some irritation, anxiety, and upset, but did you ever think that it might all be set up that way—just to help you grow, just to help you take another good look and reach just another step higher?

We learn from our experiences in this world, and we often learn most effectively from the negative experiences. It's not necessary, but sometimes when things are going well, we tend to get a little complacent and a little sluggish in our approach to life. Then something comes in that upsets us, that shakes us up, and we may stop taking things for granted and move into greater discipline and control—and lift even higher than before.

The force of the earth is primarily negative, and the force of the Divine is positive. Ultimately, the positive force will prevail, but you must learn what the divine laws are and how to apply them if they are to be effective for you here and now, in the physical world.

As you begin to work with the ideas presented in this book, you may discover many techniques that work for you. If something doesn't work for you, have the wit to let go of it and move to that which does work. And if you find that you are having some difficulty precipitating the health, wealth, and happiness that you want, you might want to apply some of the ideas that have been presented here. They have worked for a lot of people. They can work for you, too, if you work them.

Here is a thought to contemplate: The physical body, the emotional body, and the mental body all grow by taking. The physical body takes in food, the emotional body takes in comfort, and the mental body takes in information. The spiritual body grows by giving — giving of the physical energy to others, giving of the emotional caring to others, and giving of the mental energies to others in the form of guidance. Truly, as we sow, we reap. We need to maintain our balance physically, emotionally, mentally, and spiritually, and each person must determine for himself or herself where that balance is.

8

Success with Integrity

"When you do have a great deal of money,
you'll be able to enjoy what money can buy,
which includes physical objects, as well as
the joy that results when using money for the
upliftment of yourself and others."

It is important to know what we mean by *success* and *integrity*. To some people, success is having a great deal of money, being free, having loving relationships, or feeling good about themselves and their lives. Are these mutually exclusive? I don't think so. It's possible to have all of them, depending upon your choices and your willingness to focus, commit, sacrifice, and share. For me, having a great deal of money without feeling good about myself would be of little value. In order for me to feel good about myself, I need to express my caring for others by action. My experience is also that when I balance my inner needs with my outer expressions, integrity and success are in balance and create a kind of self-perpetuating, nourishing energy.

Inherent in this idea, then, is creating financial success with care and consideration for others. That doesn't mean to ignore competitive bidding or pricing or not to get something at the most effective cost. At the same time, you can do all the things that are required to make your life a *balanced* success, so that if and when you do have a great many possessions, they won't possess you. When you do have a great deal of money, you'll be able to enjoy what money can buy, which includes physical objects, as well as the joy that results when using money for the upliftment of yourself and others.

I have heard the word *integrity* used by companies as part of advertising campaigns and by nonprofit organizations encouraging the expression of integrity on a particular day, and I have also heard it used by individuals as a personal creed. I support integrity on any and every level, particularly when it awakens the value of caring for yourself and others. And it always starts with you. The greatest value of integrity can be when you decide that everything you do will be your personal expression of individual integrity.

Imagine having inner freedom sexually, physically, emotionally, mentally, and financially. This is freedom in the sense that none of those things runs *you* because you determine your expression in these areas within the guidelines of not hurting yourself and not hurting others. It is freedom to express in any and all of those areas, but whether you do or not is *your* choice, not "theirs." Lust, anger, or greed will not run you. That's a good part of the personal integrity I'm talking about — part, but not all of it.

The other part is to support your personal choices of freedom in your relationships with others and, in fact, in all that you do. That is, your behavior "out there" will match the inner freedom you have determined for yourself. When you have matched your inward freedom with your actions with every person and in every situation, something else appears. Although that "something else" may seem intangible, it is real enough to be part of a formula for your success. It is something that is whole and complete, an integer, something that cannot be divided—thus, integrity. Imagine a person who cannot be divided against himself or herself, who will not think one thing, say something else, and act in a way that reflects neither. Since he or she wouldn't believe in one thing and do another, there is no conflict of principles, so the person would not need a reason to lie. Would something be missing? Yes, inner conflict or "war" going on inside.

With integrity, an inner form of support comes forward, and from that comes a gift you have created for yourself. When you live from the inner place of integrity and reflect that out into the physical world, the inner gift is automatic. Just as virtue is its own reward, so is integrity its own reward.

We're all familiar with being obedient to an enforceable law, but imagine being obedient to an unenforceable law: the integrity, the honesty within you. No one can force you to live up to the best within yourself; no one can make you obey your conscience. Imagine doing those things because you choose to.

What does personal integrity have to do with success? (And I'm talking about inner *and* outer success, success in feeling good about yourself as well as success in having external abundance.) Integrity gives a person the strength, the courage, and the daring to take chances. Welcoming the challenges and taking risks are part of the process of success. Integrity gives you the confidence to be bold and to do the things that will produce successful results, although the results may not always be in the mainstream. To be the same as others is not always the key to success. Nor is it necessarily to be different. The choice of integrity is to go with the sound of your own drummer. How will you know if that sound is for you or deceptively against you? If you are thinking, speaking, and acting from that inner place of integrity, the chances are excellent that your choices will support your success and that you will be expressing care and consideration for others at the same time.

Will the success reveal itself and manifest immediately? As stated in previous chapters, the manifestation is something you and Spirit set into motion. The timing is likely to be influenced by your imagination, daring, and persistence. Integrity often shows up as a kind of singleness of purpose, a tenacity that endures until the end. What is the end? Your goal and, of course, your success.

People of integrity seem to have a kind of built-in ability to handle whatever comes up as they go toward success. You see, when you act from integrity, you don't lie. When you don't lie, you have no need to remember. When you don't have anything to remember, you don't have to save your energy for protection, in fear of being found out; then you have access to all your energy in the present. When you have your energy present, here and now, you are in a better position to handle whatever comes up. If you do that often enough, you'll gain an enormous amount of self-confidence, a belief in yourself based on empirical evidence — your life. When you live a life of integrity, your success may very well manifest as wealth in friendships, trust, admiration, respect, and the ability to inspire others.

You may say, "I see the value of integrity. Now, how can I acquire it as my tool, as an expression as automatic as my next breath?" Obviously, you can't order a pound of integrity, no matter how much money you have. Is there a way to get it, use it, and have it as yours? Sure there is. We get integrity through *practice*.

Practice honesty. Imagine going through one entire day without lying. We may think we do that already, but when a clerk makes an error and gives us too much change, do we always return it? When we make a personal phone call from the office, do we tell the company to charge us for it? When someone tells us some negative gossip about another, do we repeat it to someone else? We may think, "But those are such little things." Yes, they are, but if we are interested in having success, it's important to remember that integrity breeds success, so we need to start with the little things and expand from that.

I know some people who advocate world peace and prosperity, but literally in their own backyard, they are fighting with their neighbors over three feet of land and are spreading vicious lies about them. We cannot have peace in the world if we don't first start in our own backyards. Similarly, we cannot have and enjoy integrity and success on a larger scale unless we live that integrity in our personal lives. As you practice the discipline of integrity—and it does take discipline—on the personal, smaller-scale levels, you can develop the habit and apply it in all areas of your life.

A nice thing about a positive habit is that it grows stronger and stronger and eventually supports you without your even knowing it. I have a friend who had to develop a habit of not-smoking, in order to transcend a 30-year habit of smoking. He practiced not-smoking every day, sometimes a dozen times an hour. Some people were smoking, and his habit was the action of not-smoking. Now, after 12 years of not-smoking, if he lights up a cigarette (and he does occasionally), he gets nauseated and dizzy and puts it out immediately. His positive habit of not-smoking has so taken root in his psyche and body that it now supports him. It is similar with practicing integrity: As you do so, you will be supported and rewarded more than you might anticipate.

Many people claim integrity when they are actually trying to manipulate people to support their position, which they put forward as "the" moral, ethical point of view. That really isn't integrity, and those kinds of positions often have less to do with ethics than emotions, less to do with morality than ego. You don't have to fight people who do this. All you have to do is just stay present with what you know.

Similarly, for yourself, I suggest avoiding the trap of using the concept of integrity as a club. For example, when you disagree with someone, you don't need to resort to, "I'm coming from a place of integrity! How could you disagree with me?" Or the other side of that coin is, "You just don't have any integrity." Instead of keeping someone else's integrity-inventory, you can just keep practicing your own integrity. This will strengthen you to stand up inside yourself—not as a threat to others or as a defense mechanism, but as an ability to express from your heart within your current understanding.

When you recognize the integrity that lives in your heart and match it with your thoughts, you are well on your way to creating an inner life of joy and abundance. Then when you match those thoughts with the actions of integrity, the likelihood is that all aspects of your life, from intimate relationships to finances, will come into balance. From the foundation of integrity, you can have joy, abundance, and success on all levels.

9

Ten Steps to Personal Success

"If you want to create an opportunity to bring forward your success, loving is the most powerful beam for it to ride in on."

There are many different approaches to the same goal. And many of them work. What I share in this book is based on my personal experience and on observing thousands of others in their life expressions. There is a saying, "Different strokes for different folks." That reminds me of another folk saying, "There are many ways to skin a cat." I recognize that there is not just one way that works. The best thing is for you to search for, create, discover, and use the method that works for you at a particular time. How will you know what is working for you? In time, the approach will bear tangible results. If the results do not match up with what you want, then either the method doesn't work for you or you haven't worked it. What I mean by "you haven't worked it" is that perhaps you didn't really focus and apply the methodology with the persistence and endurance required. Maybe you quit early. Or maybe you did everything you could, and it still didn't work for you. If the latter is applicable in your case, have the wit to let go of what doesn't work for you and move to another approach that may very well be for your advancement.

You can change approaches, but I suggest that you don't flit from one to another, not giving each a fair chance. Sometimes, a particular approach may work for a period of time; then you may have come to a greater understanding within you, requiring a different approach. You don't have to obligate yourself to something in the past or think you're a failure because you may not have achieved the desired results — yet. Instead, you can look on your life as an experiment in seeking the formula that will eventually produce the results you want. As you do this, be patient with yourself. As long as you continue to breathe in and out, you will have ample opportunities to move toward the success you yearn for.

In chapter three, I outlined eight steps to prosperity. These have worked for many people across the planet when they applied the steps and made them part of their lives. And just to make sure that I support the idea of "different strokes," here is a ten-step variation on specific methods and approaches to your own success.

1. Focus on What You Want

Make sure you are really interested in what you want. If you have just a casual want, which generally describes a possibility ("I don't know . . . I wouldn't mind living happily ever after"), that is unlikely to produce the results you want. If, however, you start with a specific thing that has a high priority *for you,* this improves your chances. It's important that this has a high priority for you. You don't need to figure out your priority based on what you think you should want, what you think your parents think you should want, or society's standards, but on what *you* want. For some people, a high priority might be a fulfilled relationship with a husband or wife, a nourishing relationship with a child, a living relationship with the truth within them, or simply a great red sports car.

Any and all of them are fine. The important thing is to determine which one has the highest priority for you right now, which one is really important to you, and then focus on that. By focus, I mean be very specific, which leads into the next step.

2. Use Your Creative Imagination

In your mind's eye, imagine, as specifically as possible, what your goal looks like, smells like, and sounds like and even what the experience might be when achieved. If it's something like a car, imagine (or image-in) the color, the make, the feel of the leather-bound steering wheel, how it handles on the turns, the hoods on the lights going up at night, and even the smell of the interior. This same kind of specific application of your creative imagination can be used for whatever your particular want is.

3. Have Enthusiasm

Part of this word's meaning is that the energy of truth comes in, creating a powerful support system for getting what you want. You can enthusiastically support your creative imagination by visualizing the fulfillment of your want. If we continue to use the car example, then you might visualize driving with friends and/or a lover in your car, on a beautiful day, in a perfect setting. As you continue to put energy *with enthusiasm* into the visualization of the dream as a possible reality, you will be unconsciously aligning other forces within you to move things from possible to appearing.

4. Have Single-Mindedness of Purpose

Make sure that nothing else comes along to distract you. For example, putting into action steps 1 through 3 above, you may already be saving a certain amount of money every week toward your goal of owning the sports car. If you notice that there is a television sale going on, and you always wanted to change from a 20-inch to a 27-inch TV, you might take a certain amount of money — originally saved for the car — so you can buy the TV set. But doing this can dissipate the energy that has been moving toward what you originally set out to do. If you are tempted, I suggest you go back to step number 1 and *focus on what you want.* If you find that you are still preoccupied with the TV set, then perhaps what you wanted, as the *highest* priority, was not really the car. If that is the case, then you have the opportunity to reevaluate things. If it's just a matter of having a larger appetite than what you can now afford, focus again on what you want, and hold off on the TV set until you fulfill your higher priority.

On a personal level, someone's highest priority might be a fulfilled relationship with their husband or wife. A distraction might be making a choice that takes away from the relationship (these choices are sometimes called lust, greed, and selfishness). The same process applies here. Go back to number 1 and *focus on what you want.* If you do that and if you truly recognize that your wants are not frivolous but deeply meaningful, that will lead you to the next step.

5. Desire Your Want Above Everything Else

That's what I meant before by choosing the highest priority. For this step to work effectively, it's not even a matter of highest priority; it's more an issue of "this is *it.*" Another way of saying that might be, Focus on what you want and want what you focus on 100 percent.

6. Have Faith

I am not talking about religious faith, where you have faith in the divine powers. Earlier I suggested that you not make divine forces the "great bellhop in the sky," so I definitely do not suggest you pray to get a car. I suggest you let the Divinity care for divine things. You can handle this level well enough; in fact, each of us can continually learn to handle this physical level even better than we have before.

The faith I am talking about (and have mentioned in earlier sections of this book) is involved in action. I am not a big fan of trying to wish, hope, or worry something into being because this rarely, if ever, works. Through experience, I do know that when we put our faith into doing, the action of faith*ing* is a powerful step toward achieving a goal.

7. Do the Work That Is Required

The expression used earlier, "There are no free lunches," means that you need to *do* what is required to get what you want more than anything. And for all of us, ignorance of the requirements is no excuse. It is part of our responsibility to learn what is required. For example, if a person saves enough money to buy a car but does not have enough to pay for the tax, license plate, and insurance, then they haven't done the work required to fulfill their dream. In order to make the dream a reality, we must learn what is required, be ready to do it, and then do it.

Some people have a great want that is far more difficult than getting a car. I know of one young man who wanted to be a physician, be a musician, and have a great sports car — in that order. He did the work required. He went to college and medical school and then interned, an arduous commitment. While he studied medicine, he also played a musical instrument with a performing group. He graduated near the top of his class, served his internship, and is now a major contributor in an emergency ward in a hospital. He also bought a new sports car and continues to play his music. But make no mistake about it; in order to accomplish his goals, he was willing to do all the previous steps, including the work required, with great interest, focus, enthusiasm, a "faithing" that he could make it happen, and a willingness to do whatever it took.

He didn't complain — during the difficult years — that he wasn't getting enough sleep; he didn't spend time wishing that medical school only required one year of study. He didn't fight the conditions. He accepted what was going on and found joy in the challenge. When one works and studies with acceptance and joy, the retention ability is much higher than when one works in resistance and complaints.

8. Give Up All Things Opposing Your Goals

For example, my young friend, while studying to be a doctor and a musician, also had a girlfriend who complained that he was spending too much time studying and not enough time with her, so he had a choice. From the point of view of nurturing the relationship, her complaints were legitimate. So he had to go back to number 1 (Focus on What You Want) to determine, once again, his priorities. It was clear to him that being a doctor and musician was what he wanted, and he sacrificed the relationship because it was opposed to his goals. I am not saying a personal relationship is wrong. It's just that in this case, in order to make the relationship work, he would have had to take time away from his number one priorities, thus dissipating his chances for successfully achieving them. (Similarly, the woman, too, had the opportunity of evaluating her priorities, making the decision mutual to leave the relationship because her priorities were different from his.)

Either party could have changed their priorities, and as long as they were willing to handle what came with the choices, that would be fine, too. For instance, he could have dropped being a musician and spent time with his girlfriend. Or, if the woman chose, she could have made his priorities her priorities, and she might have temporarily sacrificed her personal needs to serve him during this long tenure of study. She could have helped him with his studies, given him massages during the exhausting hours of internship, and so on.

What would she get out of it? Did you ever choose to serve someone else 100 percent and do it? If you try it, you may discover that you get as much as the person you're serving—perhaps more.

In this particular case, I am talking about two human beings I know and a situation in which the woman might choose to focus on serving the man. I also endorse the man serving the woman, as a marvelous opportunity for the man to awaken to that gentle quality of nurturing another. Up until recently, that quality has been called "feminine." Why deprive men of such a rich expression? Perhaps we can all learn nurturing and recognize that it even transcends gender because it is really a higher quality.

As another example of not letting anything get in the way of what you want in personal relationships, let's take another couple, who have done all the eight steps, by focusing on each other with enthusiasm, knowing they want a relationship above all else, having the faith to know they'll get married someday, and involving themselves in the "faithing" by courting. They do what is required in terms of finances, living quarters, and so on before they get married, and then they finally do get married. Do they live happily ever after? Not unless they continually apply these steps.

Once you have what you want, you still need to work to keep it. Only it's less a matter of *keeping it* than *expanding with it.* For our loving, married couple, perhaps they have one child or more. We all know the tremendous amount of focus a newborn baby requires, and that sometimes takes time away from the personal relationship of the adults. Notice that I said "adults" not "parents." That's because it's very important that the mother and father also remind themselves that they are adults with needs in relationship to each other, not just in relationship to the children. Certainly, you can fulfill your relationship with your children responsibly, but not to the detriment of taking away adult time with each other. It's called maintaining the necessary balance.

9. Claim That You Have It

To do this, you almost play a game with yourself, pretending that you have already achieved your goal. Whether it's the car, a medical degree, and/or a personal relationship, have such confidence that you behave as if it's already yours, instead of living in anxiety that you might not get it. Now, this will probably not work for you if you do it independently of steps 1 through 8. When you've done these steps, however, the feeling of having it can be so close that you almost taste it, so you may as well put out that energy of accomplishment, or positive anticipation, which results from doing what it takes to make it happen. That energy will create an invisible path, a channel for your success to flow in and for your wants to manifest as reality.

10. Be Grateful for What You Have

With gratitude comes appreciation and, most important, *loving*. If you want to create an opportunity to bring forward your success, loving is the most powerful beam for it to ride in on. When we are more and more loving, we attract loving energy. That loving energy is for our use, not abuse. It's an energy that does not work if we try to hold on to it as ours and not share it. If a person tries to keep loving energy as their own, this is like being a negative alchemist; they can turn a powerful loving force into decay. Loving energy is within you and is also a divine gift that is a powerful force supporting accomplishment, achievement, and acceptance.

These ten steps are offered as a specific, almost-scientific formula that can work if you work them:

1. Focus on what you want, what you're really interested in.
2. Use your creative imagination. Visualize what you want.
3. Have enthusiasm about what you want.
4. Have single mindedness of purpose. Know exactly what you want and let nothing distract you.
5. Desire your want above all else. Have no alternatives.
6. Have faith. Be involved, and take action toward getting what you want. "Action for satisfaction."
7. Do the work that is required. No excuses.
8. Give up all things opposing your goal. If something is opposed to your goal, go around it, over it, under it — or remove it.
9. Claim that you have it. Pretend it's yours. Experience it as though you already have it.
10. Be grateful for what you have. And be loving. *Loving is the key*. If you can get into a consciousness of loving even before you do the first step, then your loving has a focus that empowers all the steps to come.

Do you have to do these steps, one at a time, in order? I suggest that you start doing them in order, and you may find that some of them happen all at once, rather than one separate step at a time. For example, you may find yourself doing steps 4, 5, and 6 simultaneously. If there is confusion or doubt, however, just separate them, and do them one at a time.

People throughout the world have used this formula for success. Is there anything this doesn't work on? I don't know of anything. Of course, some things are easier to achieve than others, and some things may take a longer period of time to manifest. It depends on the nature of your chosen priority. It obviously takes longer to be a physician than to get a car. It's easier to buy a 27-inch television set than a five-room house.

If you go after what you want, applying and working these ten steps, you'll get it. This isn't just theory because I have living proof from more people than I can count, who have made their lives successful. Can there be failure? Not with this formula. It's not a failure prescription. Most people already know how to fail, how to fall far short of their goal, how to quit on themselves. I don't have to teach people how to do that. This is a prescription for success.

If you review these steps and if your life doesn't seem to be moving you toward your goal, take a look to see if you're skipping any steps. Make sure that you are doing each and every one in support of what you want. Are you doing number six? Do you just *say* you have faith, or are you faith*ing?* Are you getting up and *doing* those things that bring satisfaction? How do you know if this process works unless you work it? Find out the truth for yourself by being true to the process.

It's not *my* truth I encourage you to discover, but *a* truth. There are many truths. There is the truth of gravity. You don't have to believe in it. All you have to do is let go of something, and it will fall to the ground; that's the truth of gravity in action. Is there such a truth in human beings? Yes. How can you recognize it? That's an art, not a science, but one of the ways I recognize if someone is living their truth is if I see them serve others with joy, because the highest consciousness on this planet is to express oneself in loving, joyous service. You don't have to worry about being joyous. Do the service first, the loving second, and the joy comes. Do the service just to serve someone, not to get rewards, awards, or special attention. Just do it to assist someone. In serving, you also create a clear channel for the loving energy of Spirit to work with and through you, thus creating more and greater opportunities for your own success.

There is also the truth of happiness, but that, of course, is relative. To some, happiness is a two-car garage, a white picket fence, two "perfect" kids, a color TV set, and a "perfect" marriage. That kind of happiness doesn't really exist because perfection is just not available on this planet; it wasn't designed that way. My experience of happiness is not as complex. Happiness in my life is being free from wanting anything from anybody. That doesn't mean I don't have loving relationships that are mutually supportive, but we all do things from choice, not from expectations or demand. I allow everyone around me to be free. What if they do things I don't like? I can walk away, and the same opportunity exists for them.

I don't have to have or do something in order to be happy. I don't have to go any place to be happy. Happiness is not a destination or an object. To me, it's an ongoing process that either constantly renews itself or, at times, is renewed by things I consciously do to renew it. What are some of the things I do that support happiness? I indulge in the luxury of just being me, and I only do things that make me feel good about being me. Some might say that's selfish. Well, if you break down the word, one meaning of "ish" is "relating to or being," so being myself isn't so bad. I am selfish enough not to do or say negative things to myself or others. I don't knowingly create problems for myself; as a result, what I'm left with is just me, and that's just fine. Am I special? Yes, as are all human beings.

A large part of your success lies in making it just fine to be you. And if your behavior doesn't bring happiness, you have the option of changing it. You don't have to judge it, criticize it, or make yourself wrong, but just observe your behavior, see that it may not be working for you, and give yourself the option and opportunity of changing. What greater success can you have than being happy with yourself?

10

Using Your Energy Effectively

"When you make the positive choice by making room for others as well as yourself, you are casting yourself in a role that can lead you to wealth, inner and outer."

A great part of our success has to do with clarifying what we want and what we're ready to do to get it. Some people think that their purpose on this planet is to make money; others, to "live happily ever after"; and still others, to be of service to their fellow man and woman. My theory is that we—all of us—are here to fulfill our individual plan of unfoldment. What is there, once we have unfolded? Our true wealth, which is beyond what you might think of as success. And each of us will find the wealth awaiting us according to our own rate of progress, as we seek our particular way. Or, as the song goes, "I'll do it *my way*." Of course, sometimes "my way" is not the only way; in fact, it may not always be the most effective or easiest way. Nevertheless, each of us has the inherent right to do it "my way," regardless of considerations.

An interesting thing is that *each of us* has a way that definitely leads to success and fulfillment. Then why aren't most people leading successful, fulfilled lives? Because somehow "my way" got caught up in ego and negative expressions, such as anger. There is a saying: "Those whom the Devil wants to destroy, he first makes angry." And another: "The only thing that burns in hell is the ego." I know of one writer/director in Hollywood who has had opportunity continuously knock on his door for 25 years. For most of those years, he let his anger and ego run him so much that he couldn't hear or see the opportunities presenting themselves. Instead of cooperating with the possibilities for abundance and success that were presented, he built invisible walls of judgment, impatience, and anger, all under the guise of being right. His recent unfoldment has been to be abundant financially, successful artistically, and fulfilled spiritually. By putting his focus on making others wrong, so he could be right, he had—for years—managed to bypass the opportunities for wealth and reward.

Some of you reading this may be thinking, "That's really stupid. I wouldn't do that. Just give me the chance, and I'll run with it all the way to the bank." I wonder. Have you ever gone through a period of intense frustration, where you were ready to explode or wished the other person who "caused" your frustration would explode? If so, you could have been bypassing an opportunity for your success. If the truth were known, no one "out there" actually causes our frustrations. It's each of us—by using the incident, personality, or failed expectation—who creates the emotional response, otherwise known as frustration. What we are really saying is, "I'm not getting my way." If that's all we did, that could be information. But when we add our own personal disturbance, we may be bypassing success.

How could someone not living up to your expectations assist you toward success? Do you think that the road to your abundance is lined with people, businesses, and financial institutions all ready to do what you want, when you want, wherever you want? Of course not. Everyone has their own motivations, and many have hidden agendas, otherwise known as unconscious judgments. And most people insist on doing it "my way," which may not be in accord with *your* way. So what do you do? Erupt in frustration, or move into a greater intelligence by cooperating with what is? Why should you cooperate with something you don't like? So you can succeed. Instead of regarding something as an impassable obstacle, you can use it as a stepping-stone.

For example, if you live in a house near beautiful woods, that could be quite nice. But suppose there is a dry season, no rain for many months, and then, as a result of someone's carelessness, a fire is started. The forest fire threatens and eventually burns your house. What do you do then? Curse the person who was careless as you stomp around the ashes of your memories? Or get it together, step by step, and call your insurance company, decide whether you want to rebuild there or move to another location, and get on with your life. Once you "get on with your life," you'll have the opportunity to learn that a physical object, even something as beautiful as your home by a forest, has no hold over you and that your freedom is within you, not attached to any physical or inanimate object. If you do, indeed, learn that, you will have an incredible source of power, which can be used to accomplish anything you choose.

If someone doesn't do what you ask or expect, you can use that as a stepping-stone into patience and cooperation, and you can appreciate that someone else's "my way" may be as good as your way. If you do that, you are taking another powerful step toward success within yourself and in this world. Too many times, people give vent to their emotional responses, which is a way to ignore wealth knocking at their door. It usually works much better to recognize an unpleasant experience as an opportunity to grow and learn. When you do that, you are leaning into the abundance that might be just around the bend of that experience. It's extremely valuable for you to accept that other people are constantly contributing to your life, whether you agree with their approach or not. Albert Einstein once said, "A hundred times a day I remind myself that my inner and outer life depends on the labors of other men, living and dead, and that I must exert myself in order to give in the same measure as I have received and am receiving."

The point so eloquently stated by Einstein is that each of us has the opportunity to express ourselves in one of two ways: Einstein's choice was positive; the other choice is negative. When you make a positive choice by making room for others as well as yourself, you are casting yourself in a role that can lead you to wealth, inner and outer. Will things always be clear or logical? Rarely. As long as there are human beings around, we can usually expect diverse behavior in human beings. For example, you can tell a man that there are 300 billion stars in the universe, and it's likely that he'll believe you. But if you tell him a bench has just been painted, he usually has to touch it to be sure. Human beings are funny, strange, weird, wonderful, supportive, competitive, ridiculous, and loving. When you make room for other people's success as well as your own, you'll discover the loving more often. In the loving is the key to your wealth.

Loving can be either an expression that you nod your head to or something that you put into action. If you choose to put it into action, then that requires *communication*. Within the area of communication is *acknowledging any broken promises.* That gets to be more difficult for some people because their ego and emotions are involved. They think that if they admit they broke a promise, they are "bad," "wrong," or "not worthy"; therefore, they don't admit it. The thing is, whether they realize it or not, there is a knower within them that is totally aware that they broke an agreement.

If you have any broken agreements, they are taking a great deal of your energy. Why waste your energy that way? It is much more effective for you to clean that up. Sometimes it's a simple, "Forgive me, but I promised to get this report to you by Monday, and I just won't be able to do it. Can we renegotiate?" It would serve you to take the responsibility for a broken agreement before someone else has to call it to your attention. When you acknowledge a broken promise, that doesn't make you bad. In fact, it clears the air between you and that other person. It gives you back the energy you might have been using for guilt or to hide, so that you can use it positively.

To hide a broken agreement, we may make up an excuse that is not true. When I was very young, we children would sometimes not go to school when expected, and we made up very imaginative and drastic excuses. Sometimes we said we had a high fever; other times, we said something like, "My grandmother died." Adults often do the same thing when they don't perform according to their own or someone else's agreements. If you have done this, it's important that you *clear up any broken agreements or falsehoods.* That, too, may be difficult because your ego or sense of worthiness may suffer when you admit a lie. It takes great maturity to be able to say, "What I said was untrue. I wasn't really busy. I just forgot. Please forgive me." And then you're through with it. You have been honest and have cleared up the lie between you and the other person.

Part of clearing can also include *sharing anything that you have held hidden or secret from another person that they need to know.* How can you determine if they need to know it? If it keeps coming into your mind, disturbing you emotionally and distracting you mentally, then it might be better if you shared it and cleared the air. These "withholds" can be done face to face, sometimes in writing, and sometimes, if the person is not available on those levels, in your heart. A withhold isn't necessarily bad. You can give someone information that can improve communication. You can tell someone they have bad breath, and they may take a breath mint or brush their teeth. That simple. Sometimes you may withhold your loving appreciation. It is valuable for the other person to know that you care for him or her — not necessarily on a romantic level, but as a beautiful human being.

By doing those things that facilitate clear communication, you are also clearing the way for wealth to pour forth in personal and business relationships. As you are "cleaning up your act," you may find yourself literally cleaning up your living quarters, your desk, your office, and your car. That gives you a better opportunity to *organize and maintain your life* to support your abundance. It's no mistake that the largest, most successful corporations are usually very effective and efficient because they have taken steps to achieve a high level of organization, and they maintain it by constant attention. Keep your records accurate, from your checkbook to your files. Pay bills on time, and the chances are that you, too, will be paid on time. On a business level and on a one-to-one level, fulfill your commitments. This will permit a kind of personal closure, so again, there are no undone things pulling on your energy.

For you to work your life successfully, it's important that you *make agreements and agree to guidelines that support you* in business and personal relationships and that you *keep them*. It would not be for your advancement to agree to something that is impossible to do, just because you want to please someone else. If your boss asks you to lunch, and you already have a luncheon appointment with a client, it would be foolish to say yes to both. Make sure that these agreements are understood by all parties involved. This way, there will not be regrets or resentments in the relationships. If there are, I encourage you to quickly *discuss any regrets or resentments* to get clarity and, if necessary, renegotiate to get a balanced agreement.

All these actions contribute to giving you the gift of your power. That which takes away or subverts your energy, dissipates the power within you. Completions, fulfillment of agreements, and closure—all are actions that support your being present, here and now, using the energy of mind, body, and Spirit for your own success.

11

Awareness and Choice

"The love of another person can support you in your search and discovery, but it is you who has to experience your own self-worth."

A premise of this book is that we *are* intended to have joy and abundance in our lives. It's as if we have a vertical channel within us that is designed for abundance to flow through. Even though health, wealth, and happiness are a distinct possibility in our lives, we also have to recognize that such a balanced state is not a common occurrence for most people most of the time. Yet I know, by my life and the lives of hundreds of other friends and colleagues, that such a life not only is possible but has already manifested.

The challenge is not so much tuning in to the "channel" of abundance in your life, but removing those things that are blocking the flow of success. Suppose that this channel is like a vertical canal, and rather than the waters of wealth flowing through you, canal locks have been erected that stop the flow. These locks (or blocks) can actually deter or stop the flow of richness intended for your life. Who put these blocks there? There can be many explanations. In psychological terms, we could say that "the iniquities of the parents were visited upon the children" when you, as a child, may have unconsciously accepted some of your parents' limitations and negative conditioning. These early blocks can take on weight and size, until they become rooted in emotional and mental cement.

Perhaps some of you may have been born with imbalances, and the choice is to dissolve or otherwise remove these blocks or to let them remain and, perhaps, become rooted. How does a person get rid of the blocks, remove the "locks," so the abundance can flow? All the techniques and steps described in previous chapters are intended to keep that channel clear for the joy to flow through your life.

Some of you may have created new blocks, as recently as yesterday, by indulging in such expressions as greed, lust, anger, and extreme emotions. Emotions can often be huge blocks, deterring or stopping the flow of success that is intended for you in this lifetime. Most people live a life that is full of emotional content. That doesn't mean that the emotional content is always negative. You can feel good or bad, up or down, lost or found. And many people act and react from how they are feeling, making their lives go up and down like an elevator or Yo-Yo.

Regardless of what is going on in your life externally, if you validate everything through your emotions, you are likely to interpret situations through your emotions and react accordingly. I know of a man who got into a fist fight because his shirts were not returned from the laundry on time. I know of another man who, while driving, was shot at by another driver who thought he was going too slowly. Shirts and driving speed as occasions for physical violence! Absurd, isn't it? But then again, when people live life through their emotions, almost anything is possible.

Now, those are extreme cases and you, of course, may think they have little to do with you. This process can be subtle, however. Have you ever handled some external circumstance in ways that were too extreme for the actual event? Did you ever quit a job because of emotional upset, without having enough money in the bank to cover your month's rent? I am not saying that leaving a job is wrong, just that if you had been able to rise above your emotions, you might have done something more sensible, such as looking for another job while you were still employed. Did you ever erupt in anger at your mate over an issue, ready to leave or get a divorce, and hours later you were apologizing and loving each other? And you may recall instances in your life where your reaction was stretched to the limit — not because of the event but because of the emotional charge you put on the event.

Why be a victim of your emotions? Why not stop yourself before responding from your emotions? People who live mainly from their emotions often act as judge, jury, and executioner. They emotionally, mentally, and sometimes physically do great harm to others (and themselves) based on their emotional content rather than proof. A fair jurisprudence system is based on "innocent until proven guilty." Those who act out of emotions come from a conditioned place where guilt and judgment are built in, and they usually take little time to determine if there is sufficient proof to be critical of another.

If you're interested in removing blocks to your success, it is important that you deal with any emotional reactions you have. It could be naive for us to think that, just by reading this, you can eliminate blocks immediately. But you can start doing something, right now, about dissolving any blocks to your abundance. The first thing to do is to recognize what is going on inside you in relationship to another person or condition. Recognize, not react. The recognition can be as simple as saying, "I don't like that." For example, have you ever "gone crazy" in traffic? I know some people who really go to the edge emotionally when caught in a traffic jam. Even though there may be bumper-to-bumper cars as far as the eye can see, some people lean on their horns in fury, as if the sound of their horns will make all the cars suddenly move. How can you handle a situation like that? The first thing to do is recognize what is going on: "Traffic is jammed, and I don't like it. In fact, if this goes on much longer, the way I am, I'll blow up."

Notice that the above example is one of recognition of the possibility of blowing up, not indulgence in the emotional reaction of blowing up. After the recognition, then what? Now comes awareness of choice and, as stated in previous chapters, choosing your choice. You have recognized (become aware that) you are stuck in traffic and are ready to respond emotionally. Now, what are you going to do about it? Blow your horn? In awareness, you know that doing this will not help ease the traffic jam.

What other choices are available? For one, you can inch your car to the right-hand lane and, in time, get off that particular road and take a more circuitous route. "But that would add a half hour to my journey," you might think. That's a good awareness. There are always other choices. In this case, do you want to inch along the highway, in case it will eventually clear up, or are you willing to add a half hour by taking a bypass route? Know this: Either choice is fine. You don't need to judge your choices. You can just evaluate them and choose.

On what basis do you make the choices? Again, in awareness. For example, if you're aware that you have a short emotional fuse, taking the bypass route may be for you. Even if it adds an extra half hour, if driving in moving traffic is easier for you, then do it. If you would rather gamble that the traffic will clear and save yourself that half hour, then make the choice, and make subsequent choices to support the first decision. While you're inching along, you can put on the radio or a music tape that is particularly soothing. One friend of mine, whenever he gets tense, listens to a tape of a guitarist playing Bach fugues, and that eases his tension. And, if this traffic condition occurs often, you can make a third choice. You can leave at a different time or even arrange to go to a different destination until traffic clears. Some people have chosen to move in order to avoid driving a particular route during rush hour every day.

The traffic jam is a concrete example of the "jams" we have in our lives. By recognizing what the jam or block is, you have the opportunity to make any number of choices. Any choice that is other than an emotional reaction can contribute to dissolving any blocks that impede your success. You don't think that a traffic jam might impede your success? How about being stuck in traffic for an hour and a half and getting to work late? You may be upset because you needed that time to complete a project; your temper may be frayed, so when your boss asks you about the report, you may respond in a curt, impatient, defensive manner. This kind of a response can ultimately limit your success. One important strategy is to make a positive choice *before* a negative event, whenever possible. For example, instead of leaving things to the last minute on the assumption that all other things will fall into line (such as traffic), you can choose to finish the project a day or two before it is due. Or, if you're late when you come in, the first thing you can do is recognize your tension and take a moment to calm down. Then you can tell your boss about the traffic and renegotiate — without emotional content — more time to complete the report.

You'll know you are doing this "awareness-choosing" technique successfully when you take *full responsibility* for what is going on in your life, inside and outside. If you find yourself responding, "I hate him," or "She makes me crazy," then you are involved in "internal exteriorization," making someone or something outside yourself the cause of your internal reaction. You have set up a premise that if that particular person leaves or that particular situation changes, your difficulties will also disappear. Some people get involved in personal relationships and separate many, many times; others get a job, quit a job, and change jobs many, many times. Many people live that kind of existence, blaming him or her, this or that, and get furious or despondent over life, having alibis and excuses for why their existence is not one of health, wealth, and happiness.

It's so easy to fall into, "If only he would . . . if only she could . . . ," putting all the responsibility on an external source. In that position, not only do we solve nothing but we also create a feeling of powerlessness within ourselves because we have created a situation that, by definition, we can do nothing about. If it's all "their fault," then we are victims of "their faults." Those who live according to that *modus operandi* often experience feelings of failure and a sense of worthlessness.

If you live in a reactive consciousness where external stimuli determine how you respond, you are depriving yourself of creating and experiencing your own immediate success. Every time you blame someone else for your life, you are giving them the power to run your life, even if they haven't asked for it. If you don't like the way someone is doing something, instead of blaming and criticizing, you can make other choices. You can assist, teach, and train someone to do better. If you offer such information in a loving consciousness, the chances of your success are good. If you offer information with impatience and judgment, the chances may be limited.

We are living in an age of great possibilities of awareness. If you have a problem that is unknown to you, it usually runs you in some way, and there is little you can do about it except react. For example, when you have physical discomfort and don't know what's causing it, your body is responding to an unknown imbalance. The imbalance can be caused by any number of things, ranging from physical to emotional. When you go to a doctor, it is so that you can determine the cause. Once the cause is known, treatment is recommended. Under the best of conditions, the treatment works and the ailment is cured, leaving you in balance. I suggest that you not wait until the symptoms of imbalance become so obvious that you need treatment. Why not solve the difficulty before it becomes a problem? Why not find the cure before it becomes a dis-ease?

That's why I continually stress awareness and choice. On some level, you know if something is "running you." Rather than wait to be told by the symptom — such as ulcers, a backache, a rash, cancer — you can recognize *now* what is running you and, perhaps, catch it before it manifests in physical dis-ease.

A person can be run by many things other than physical ailments, of course. If you are consistently having financial difficulties, the likelihood is that you are being run by a limiting block. If you find yourself in and out of intimate relationships, always making the other person wrong, you are probably being run by negative conditioning. If you experience your work as a sentence rather than a creative expression, you may be living a life determined by internal limitations. Does that mean that you should never change partners or a job? Not at all. It does imply, however, that you take responsibility for your choices. If you don't, you are likely to create the same old problems with new partners or new jobs.

In awareness, you can take a look at your life — your personal relationships, your finances, your vocational expressions — and see if there has been a limiting pattern. It doesn't matter if the people or events have changed; just see if there are patterns that have recurred. Quite often, people continue living a life of repeated restrictions because of the emotional content running them.

In awareness, you have the opportunity to recognize if emotions have been running your life. If so, you have the opportunity of making choices that will support change and transformation. Notice that I said "choices" again. This is not a choice just on a word level, where you recognize your reactive pattern and say that things will get better. Things do not necessarily get better just because you become aware of a problem and then say it will get better. Things don't necessarily get better even if you pray that they will. But they are likely to get better if you first take responsibility and then take action.

In awareness, you can recognize the problem or difficulty and the preferred solution. If you focus on the problem, the chances are that little will occur to improve things. If you take action by focusing on the solution, however, you have the opportunity to improve your life. For example, I know of a man who drank a few six-packs of beer each day, and in the evenings he would have a few drinks to relax. Even though he knew about the damaging effects of alcohol on some people, he felt that he was impervious to illness from it. He had yearly physical checkups, and the doctor indicated he was doing fine.

Then one day he realized that he no longer felt invulnerable. In awareness, he recognized that drinking alcoholic beverages was now harmful to his health. He made the choice to not drink anything with alcohol. It was very difficult, but he took responsibility for the choice beyond the word level. (Those who have quit just on the word level have usually quit and started many times.) He chose to first go to a retreat with about 100 other people, where no alcohol was available. He made a responsible choice in awareness. He supported his awareness that breaking such a habit would be very difficult by making a responsible choice—going to a retreat not only where alcohol was unavailable but where he would be surrounded by 99 other people who would support his change of habit. And when he returned to "normal" life, he continued to create supportive people and experiences so he could create a new habit. It wasn't a matter of his stopping drinking alcohol. In awareness, he recognized that he had to create a new habit to replace an old habit. His new habit was drinking-not. And he would not spend time with people who did drink. He didn't judge them, but he made wise choices to strengthen his new habit. He did not have alcoholic beverages in his home or permit anyone into his home with alcohol.

The point of this is to take responsibility for all aspects of your life. Do positive things, and surround yourself with people who will not necessarily agree with your conditioned point of view, but who will support an action of freedom. What is freedom? Not being attached. No hooks to alcohol and, most important, to a life of emotional content. Imagine being with supportive friends who do not support emotional, negative reactions. Imagine choosing people who do not gossip or spread rumors. Imagine choosing people and places that permit you to just be present with what is going on.

A major block in the channel of our potential success is not being present. Many of you may respond, "What do you mean, 'not being present'? Of course I'm present. Here I am." We can be physically present but pulled by our past and anxiety-ridden about our future. Many people have emotional content going in so many fields. In the dance of romance, for example, you may look at someone and picture how beautiful life will be together in that fantasy of "someday my prince (or princess) will come." That's your desire pulling you into your future, which is often a limitation of your past, as learned through your parents. What are the choices? How can you be present now without losing yourself in the future?

In awareness, again, figure out what is going on with you *inside*. As you start to go toward "your future" in the form of another person, another relationship, another financial venture, another job, or another physical location, are you going forward, *as you are right now?* Or are you going forward into fantasyville in order to escape from a feeling of loss, which may be based on past experiences? Before you get with that reactive elevator or Yo-Yo, it can help you to recognize that an external situation will not solve an internal conflict. The love of another person can support you in your search and discovery, but it is *you* who has to experience your own self-worth. If you expect that other person to give you your self-worth, the relationship may end in disharmony and divorce. If you do not do well in this job due to your own poor work-habits and resistance to supervision, you may find yourself in the same situation in another job. In personal and vocational relationships, it is *you* who has to do what it takes to discover, experience, and express your value.

Many people play a game of Ping-Pong with their lives. They make themselves the Ping-Pong ball that is hit back and forth between the paddles of the past and of the future-hope. When they get hit by the past, they are hurled toward the future-hope, only to be hit back into the past, never stopping to be present. Some people carry around guilt, self-judgment, and blame for something they did a long time ago. Wouldn't it be great if you could recognize that you don't have to blame yourself now for what you did in the past? Even if you really did something that your mother, father, teacher, husband, wife, child, colleague, or society said was "terrible," here you are right now, right at this moment, reading this book and doing something quite wonderful. What's so wonderful about this book? By itself, nothing. But you may be reading it to seek information to improve your life. Anything that improves your life is wonderful.

We often spend time on our past because it's familiar, and to many, what is familiar is comfortable and not frightening. Even if the familiar is limited and filled with negativity, at least we know what it is. Often, people unconsciously put so much energy into their past that they live today as slaves of yesterday. They may spend their lives beating themselves up because of what they did or didn't do in the past.

If you want success in your life, it's time to recognize that you cannot change the past. This isn't just 20 years ago; you can't even change what happened 20 seconds ago. You can't change things so your mother or father would have loved you the way you may have wanted them to. You can't change things in the past so you would have expressed love the way you might have wanted to. What a waste of time it is to put your energy into something that is really a bucket of ashes. The past is dead. Why continue to put energy into a ghost? The best you can do with the past is to use it as a reference point, like a scientist does with an experiment. If you need to look at it, do so with awareness. Without emotional content, see what happened; see it for information, not for blame or judgment. There may also come a time when you have no need even to look at the past. You can simply let it go immediately, so you have all your energy present for living in the present.

If you do let the past be past, then you have the present to deal with, unless, of course, you're hooked on desire and anxiety about the future. There is something you can do about your future, however. By focusing on your present, you can assist your future. By doing those things, now, that support your eventual success, your future will reflect that. Your future will someday be your present, where you will be able to reap the rewards of what you are doing now. That is why I stress being creative and courageous *now*. There is nothing wrong with asking yourself what you want in your life. Of course, that intimates that the reward is in the future. Once you recognize what you want, however, you have creative choices in the present that can make your wants into a reality.

Using your creativity, you can choose things to do and things not to do in support of what you want. It isn't so important to intellectually understand *why* you are doing something; it is more important to recognize *what* you are doing. Is what you are doing supporting your getting what you want? You may as well accept responsibility for your choice because you're stuck with it, anyhow. If you look at what you're doing and find that it is not really supportive of the success you want, your next step is simple: stop doing it. You don't have to act or respond in ways that are not for you. You don't have to be a victim of emotional content and do things that are against yourself.

If your life is not going the way you want it to go, if you are not *right now* living a life of health, wealth, and abundance, then stop, look, and listen. Stop and take a look at the things you are doing and the things you are not doing. Then go inside and listen to your inner awareness. If you do listen, you just might hear what you can do to remove blocks and let your success flow. The direction may be as specific as completing a form and mailing it in, paying a bill, answering a letter, studying for an exam, preparing a report, or celebrating someone's birthday.

Don't dismiss anything that's in the way of you and your experience of joy. If you're 1 percent off, that can create an irritation that makes your life uncomfortable. Go for what you want in your life. Support your want — envision it, write about it, read about it, and do those things in the present that pull you toward your successful future. You can create relationships in the present that contribute to your joyous future. It's not a matter of a mathematical formula. It is a matter of specific techniques, such as those described in this book, applied with courage, integrity, and loving. If you do it with loving, the flow of success can be effortless. If you do it with loving, mistakes made by you and others are just experiences. If you do it with loving, your life can be a success.

It is possible to experience physical health, spiritual richness, financial stability, and nurturing personal relationships. It's up to you. Treat yourself lovingly on the way to your success. You deserve it.

About John-Roger

For the last 25 years, John-Roger has been deeply involved in working to promote greater health, well-being, and peace. His efforts support a large number of organizations and individuals involved in education, science, health, and community service.

John-Roger is also the founder of Insight Seminars, which offers seminars to enhance personal and professional effectiveness; Baraka Center, a healing and research clinic; Heartfelt Foundation, which is committed to community service; University of Santa Monica, as well as other organizations committed to the same principles.

If you are interested in other books by John-Roger, write to Mandeville Press, P.O. Box 3935, Los Angeles, CA 90051, or call (213) 737-4055.